Praise for other books b ...

Take Control of Your Career

"An authoritative British voice in careers coaching."

Rosalind Renshaw, *The Times*

"I am delighted at the success of John Lees' book *How To Get A Job You'll Love* and find that others share my high opinion of John's practical and authoritative advice as a career coach."

Sir John Harvey-Jones MBE

"Well written, insightful and pragmatic, a 'must read' for anyone seeking to progress their career."

Jeff Grout, Business Consultant & author

"Excellent advice to help you take charge of your career and manage it positively."

Jo Bond, Joint Managing Director, Right Coutts

"Describes many of the behaviours I have repeatedly seen exhibited by successful individuals. I recommend it wholeheartedly."

Stephen Bampfylde, Chairman, Saxton Bampfylde Hever Plc

"Reveals the secrets of getting recognition and reward from your employer."

Daniel Porot, international careers expert and author of The PIE Method

"A lively and interesting guide aimed at informing and supporting individuals with career planning."

Deirdre Hughes, Director, Centre for Guidance Studies, University of Derby

"Job search within your organisation! What a great and very sensible idea. John Lees' book is packed with practical hints to progress your career from within the organization."

Robin Wood, MD, Career Management Consultants Limited

"John Lees gives practical advice to help you take control of advancing your career – now it's down to you!"

Joëlle Warren, MD of executive recruiters Warren Partners Ltd.

How to Get a Job You'll Love
2005–6 edition

"Offers a fresh look at career planning"

The Guardian

"I love its originality and thoroughness. Stimulates creative thinking and guides you thorough the job search process. We give copies to all our clients."

Dr Harry Freedman, Director, Career Energy

"Filled with exceptional wisdom and practical guidance – a thought providing tool for self-discovery and career mastery. I highly recommend."

Gayle Lantz, President, WorkMatters Executive Coaching and co-author

"John's book is a classic – comprehensive, insightful land sympathetic – it will be around for a long time."

Brian McIvor, Brian McIvor & Associates careers and training consultancy

"If you are looking for a great way to re-invent your career, read this book."

Tim Nicholson, Chief Executive, Recruitment & Employment Confederation

"Challenges you to have fun and get excitement out of your work."

Rod Howgate, Director Warren Partners

"Combines the insights of the coach and counsellor with the practical advice of the career consultant."

Liz Friedrich, Senior Manager, Mentors Counselling Consultants

Job Interviews

Job Interviews

Top Answers to Tough Questions

Matthew DeLuca and John Lees

The **McGraw·Hill** Companies

London • Boston • Burr Ridge, IL • Dubuque, IA • Madison WI • New York
San Francisco • St. Louis • Bangkok • Bogotá • Caracas • Kuala Lumpur
Lisbon • Madrid • Mexico City • Milan • Montreal • New Delhi • Santiago
Seoul • Singapore • Sydney • Taipei • Toronto

Job Interviews: Top Answers to Tough Questions
Matthew J. DeLuca and John Lees
ISBN 0077107047

 **Professional**

Published by McGraw-Hill Professional
Shoppenhangers Road
Maidenhead
Berkshire
SL6 2QL
Telephone: 44 (0) 1628 502 500
Fax: 44 (0) 1628 770 224
Website: www.mcgraw-hill.co.uk

British Library Cataloguing in Publication Data
A catalogue record for this book is available from the British Library

Library of Congress Cataloguing in Publication Data
The Library of Congress data for this book has been applied for from the Library of
Congress

Text design and typesetting by Gray Publishing
Cover design by Two Associates Ltd
Printed and bound in UK by Clays Ltd, Bungay, Suffolk

ISBN 0077107047

Adapted from Best Answers to the 201 Most Frequently Asked Interview Questions by
Matthew J. Deluca. ISBN 007016357X Copyright 1997 by McGraw-Hill Companies, Inc.

Contents

Preface

This book prepares you for one of the most important aspects of career transition: how to answer the toughest job interview questions effectively. This advice will help you whatever kind of job you are chasing – public or private sector, mainstream employer or not-for-profit organization.

The approach of the book is practical and hands-on. You should do more than just read the book. *Use it* by practising your answers, and preparing your evidence. Listen to yourself and, in the process, determine what works and what doesn't. If you don't have the evidence to support the claims you've made in your CV, and if you haven't prepared enough to cope with probing questions, you've made the classic mistake of *trying to do the work in the interview room itself.* The real work is in the preparation you do now, anticipating questions and practising your responses.

Do you have an interview today? Tomorrow morning? Help is at hand. There is a fast-track route for readers who need to fly through the book and get help on the most critical and most likely questions. Look for questions with a star (✶) next to them. Looking at these questions isn't an alternative to full preparation, but they will help you to focus on the key questions at the heart of every job interview.

How to Use This Book

This book covers 201 demanding, probing, awkward, exacting, difficult or just plain awful interview questions. If you need a quick-fix solution because you have an interview in the very near future, see the 'Fast Track' section below.

If you have a little more preparation time, decide what areas you need the most help on and tackle those first. What questions would you really hate to face? Where are you underprepared? Where do your strengths lie?

Would you like to understand more about how interviewers operate, and know some of the tricks of the trade they will use at interview? See **Chapter 1** to start you off. Not sure what you have to offer? If you don't know, there's little chance you'll convey your strengths to an interviewer. Review what you're looking for from work in **Chapter 2**.

You'd be unwise to skip the key section on preparation (see **Chapter 4**) – it contains all the things you need to do before the interview in order to be successful. You can also learn more about communicating your primary message to a decision-maker in **Chapter 6**.

Worried about how the interview is going to open? You'll find the discussion of opening questions helpful (see **Chapter 5**).

Chapters 7–13 cover the full range of questions you are likely to experience during the course of a job interview. If you have been locked up doing research for the past two years, you may need to give attention to your interpersonal skills, or to work out how your personality fits best into the workplace or team. You are recommended to look at the personality questions (see **Chapter 7**).

Are you a great manager but your technical skills are a bit rusty? Go to the questions regarding experience first (see **Chapter 10**). Have you recently qualified, or are your qualifications a little out of date? Go to the questions on education and training (see **Chapter 9**).

Many job-seekers are now facing question sequences which look in detail at your competencies. See **Chapter 11** for a full discussion of this topic. Nearly every interviewer asks difficult questions that will throw you off balance, so prepare by reviewing **Chapter 12**. You may be worried about what to do if an interviewer comes up with an illegal or unethical question (see **Chapter 13**).

Finally, we look at the final stage of the interview process (see **Chapter 14**) – what happens if you get a job offer, and what you can do if you don't.

Fast Track: How to Use This Book if You Have an Interview TOMORROW

Twenty of the questions covered by this book are given a ✱ rating. This symbol is included in the list of questions (see page x), and also against each question as it appears in the text.

These questions represent the basic toolkit – the all-important top 20 questions to prepare for in any interview. Read nothing else, and you'll still have an advantage in the interview. One final tip – don't discuss **pay** until you've read the answers to **Question 201** (see page 240).

List of 201 Questions

Chapter 6

Chapter 7

Chapter 8

Chapter 9

Chapter 10

Chapter 12

About the Authors

John Lees

John Lees, a graduate of the Universities of Cambridge and London, has spent many years training interviewers. Until 1993 he was Chief Executive of the Institute of Employment Consultants (now the Recruitment & Employment Confederation, REC). He now specializes in helping people make difficult career decisions – difficult either because they don't know what to do next, or because there are barriers in the way to success.

John has undertaken career workshops in Europe, the USA, and South Africa and currently runs a careers consultancy in the north-west of England. He writes regularly on careers matters for *The Times*, and his work has been featured widely, including *The Guardian*, *Sunday Mirror*, the *Evening Standard*, *Management Today*, *Personnel Today*, *Red*, and *Cosmopolitan*. His *How To Get A Job You'll Love* was the WH Smith Business Book of the Month in January 2003, and in the same year became the best-selling careers book by a British author. John is also the author of *How To Get The Perfect Promotion*, also published by McGraw-Hill.

He lives in Cheshire with his wife, the children's writer Jan Dean, and their two sons.

See **www.johnleescareers.com** for further materials and checklists, details of John's books and career tools, and for details of workshops and programmes run by John Lees Associates.

Matthew J. DeLuca

Matthew J. DeLuca is president of the Management Resource Group, Inc., a New York City-based consulting firm specializing in professional placement, training, outplacement, outsourcing and other Human Resources (HR) activities for major organizations in a variety of industries. Before this he held senior HR positions for World Wrestling Entertainment, Flipside, an on-line game unit of Vivendi Universal, Chemical Bank (now JPMorganChase) and the Bank of Tokyo. Matt conducts frequent workshops on career and job search efforts for several colleges, including New York University, and is invited to speak on HR topics at professional organizations throughout the United States. He is also the author of *How to Get a Job in 90 Days or Less* (McGraw-Hill), *Handbook of Compensation Management* and *Not for Profit Personnel Forms and Guidelines* (currently in its third edition).

Acknowledgements

I would like to thank Matthew DeLuca for allowing his original book *Best Answers To The 201 Most Frequently Asked Interview Questions* to be updated and revised for the UK market.

I am grateful to the many experienced recruiters, career coaches and HR professionals who over the years have informed my thinking on the job interview – from both the interviewer and the job applicant perspective. I would like to express very special thanks to my former colleagues at the REC, including Dr Ian Webb – whose insights into the inter-viewing process continue to impress and inspire.

As ever, my thanks go to my ever-diligent McGraw-Hill editor Elizabeth Choules.

This book is dedicated with love and ever-increasing appreciation to my parents, George and Mair Lees.

John Lees

Acknowledgements

(TO *BEST ANSWERS TO THE 201 MOST FREQUENTLY ASKED INTERVIEW QUESTIONS*)

Any book requires the support and assistance of a variety of individuals that, in any combination, lead to the completion of the project. At the top of my list is my extremely talented colleague, friend and wife, Nanette, who is becoming a more essential element of these projects with each project undertaken. Although not always in agreement, she certainly provides invaluable assistance in taking my ideas and making them a coherent and complete manuscript.

Also to be mentioned are Lisa Wolf, a terrific professional and a great fan, as well as Palma Mitchell, a solid human resource expert and a lot more. Also to be mentioned are the executives and employees at a unique organization – Titan Sports, Inc. – in particular Vine and Linda McMahon, as well as Dawn Lyon, all of whom have been great to work with and have helped me to gain additional insight on my job searches from a recruiter's perspective in a most challenging environment. Last let me mention Lynn Johnson and Ken Coleman (and the deceased LeVaun Eustice, before them) who have provided me with a great educational setting in which to grow professionally and an ongoing forum to develop new approaches to a variety of human resource issues, including recruiting, and to test them in the marketplace.

Last, let me thank the people at McGraw-Hill for all their interest and attention. At the top of the list is Philip Ruppel for guiding me through this aspect of my career and for what has become my sixth book. Thanks also to Betsy Brown for, one more time, taking me through the steps from book concept and proposal to successful conclusion. And to Fred Dahl for a painstaking editing of the manuscript.

Matthew J. DeLuca

Understanding the Interview Game

If you've got as far as the job interview you've done the hardest part – you've got through the initial selection process. Now you're up against a short list of people who are probably a close match in terms of experience, skills and qualifications. To get the job, you have to do two things: put in an above-average interview performance, and make sure you don't talk yourself out of the job. **The best candidate doesn't necessarily get the job: the best interviewee does.**

This book looks at the ways that top interview performances win job offers. It also helps you to anticipate the best and the worst in terms of interview questions. Ultimately, this book enables you to shine during the interview process.

Too many candidates believe that whether they perform well in an interview is more down to luck than good judgement or preparation. They are right in one sense – we manage our luck. Anticipating the questions you will be asked at interview, and communicating your 'message', is a critical part of the process of improving the odds in your favour.

The goal is a straightforward one: to identify the key questions in advance. To do the hard work of the interview long before you get anywhere near the interview room, so that when you are called on, you've done your thinking in advance. You've prepared your examples, and you've worked out your replies in outline form – not memorized in rote form, but with sufficient detail so that your reply will be clear, confident, and to the point.

The aim of this book is to prepare you for the key aspects of the interview process and to give the questions you will be asked the attention they deserve. But note: while concentrating on answering the interviewers' questions skilfully, you also need to stay alert to the non-verbal aspects of the communication process – the things you say through your body language, your tone of voice, and the way you present yourself at interview.

Why Interviews?

Effective recruitment has been described as *the right person in the right time at the right cost*. Interviews are an expensive process in terms of staff time and administration; to find the right person an employer has to make a significant time and resource commitment. There are direct and indirect costs in any recruitment process:

■ *Direct costs* are the most visible in the hiring process. These include the cost of job advertisements, placement fees paid to recruitment consultants, travel and meeting expenses, and fees paid for testing.

■ *Indirect costs* are not-so-visible costs that should be considered as well. The first is the opportunity cost that occurs – how the business loses out by not having the right person in the job. Other indirect costs include the staff time absorbed in the administration of dealing with job applications, letters of rejection, interview arrangements. Being aware of the costs of recruitment failure may give you some important leverage when it comes to the job offer.

Understanding why organizations take on this cost is an important part of your preparation process – interviews represent a significant investment of time and energy from an employer. Employers conduct interviews to discover the information that your CV doesn't provide – your attitude to work, your personality, the way you will fit into the organization and the team.

Kinds of Interviews

Screening Interviews

Whether you are presenting yourself to an agency, a recruiter or an HR department, you may be subject to a certain number of screening interviews. The 'gatekeepers' doing the interview have basic information regarding the job opening and the requirements for the position. Their function is to pass on only those candidates who appear to be a close fit for the position. They ask direct questions about your experience, education, expectations. They go over your CV with you. Depending on the experience level of the interviewer, you may be interviewed in depth. But it is of no matter that this is a low-level interview: if you do not pass the gatekeepers, then you are out. Their job is to weed out those who are inappropriate for the position. Those who 'pass' proceed to another level at the organization or, if the gatekeeper was an agency or recruiter, to the hiring organization.

Courtesy Interviews

You know when you have one of these. You've received a lead and persuaded someone to see you. You may be referred by a present employee, a client, a relative, or a neighbour – anyone who has a tie-in to the company and who could get your foot in the door. This is a great start, because organizations are far more likely to hire people they feel they know. This interview may be similar in tone to a screening interview (they may not know what to do with you and will ask a number of general questions), or you may find that you are being probed to see if you can help with a particular problem. If so, find out as much as you can about the organization's needs.

Don't forget that this kind of interview may be the opening shot in a longer series of meetings and discussions, which may lead ultimately to a job offer or may lead you to other useful connections. Remember it's always worth asking 'Who else should I be talking to?'.

A word of warning – sometimes you may be given a courtesy interview so that someone can pump you for information about what your past or present employer is doing in the marketplace. See the discussion of **Q159** in **Chapter 12** for ways of handling this.

Registration Interviews

This kind of interview is common with many recruitment agencies, but also with some employers. It is used far more often for temporary workers than for permanent jobs. This form of interview is intended to be a 'general purpose' meeting to discuss how you might fit a wide range of positions. You won't therefore be matching yourself against a single position, but offering evidence that will help a recruiter match you against a range of possibilities, either presently held or the kinds of jobs that might come up in the future. In this interview it's usually important to be very clear about the kind of work you will want to do, and your motivation to do it, particularly if this involves a job change.

Recruitment Consultancy Interviews

Sometimes these interviews are essentially Registration Interviews (see above). However recruiters will often interview you in order to assess whether you should be short-listed and put forward to an employer. It's important that you realize that you are not talking to the final decision-maker, but to an intermediary. Nevertheless, it's an intermediary who matters. A recruitment consultancy will charge the employer a fee if you are appointed, so it is important to a recruitment consult-ant that you look and sound the part if you go to a job interview. The safest bet, therefore, is to treat the intermediary as the *eyes and ears of the employer*. Dress and present yourself as if it was the final interview. And be prepared to answer some tough questions – particularly on what you have achieved, what you have to offer over other candidates, and how strong your motivation will be to accept the job if it is offered.

Stress Interviews

They exist. Unless you are looking to be head of a major urban transit system, school chancellor, or any position so inundated with stress that mere mortals need not apply, stress interviews are not common. There are ways to deal with them, as covered in detail in **Chapter 12**.

Situational Interviews

Can you think on your feet? These interviews involve '*What if…*' scenarios. The interviewer may be either trying out real-life problems on you to see what you would do or just may be in a creative mood. The interviewer is looking for empathy: Can you put yourself into another's place? How would you act? If you have the knowledge and experience on paper, the interviewer can probe to see how you run with these types of questions. At the end you might want to comment, '*Those were really intriguing questions. Do they relate to real-life situations here at ____?*'

Competency-based Interviews

A 'competency' is more than a skill. It is a combination of skill, know-how, attitude and observable behaviour. You could say that it's not just what you do, but *how* you do it.

Competency-based interviewing usually begins by defining the competencies demonstrated by above-average performers, and will then give candidates a chance to present evidence (in writing or at interview, or both) which demonstrates where and how this competency was used. Candidates are often given the opportunity to present a written statement in advance of an interview. An alternative, commonly used, is that screening interviews are conducted by telephone. When it comes to the final interview, you will still find that the questions are largely about competencies. See **Chapter 11** for a more detailed discussion of competency questions.

This book will assist you considerably with competency-based interviews because you will be encouraged to be more aware of your skills, experience and achievements. A good performance in a competency-based interview is essentially a matter of being able to talk about a time when you used a competency, what exactly you did, and what you achieved as a result.

Panel Interviews

You may be faced with several interviewers at the same time, with either one taking the lead and the others interjecting from time to time, or you may face a battery of questions from all directions. Candidates often find this approach stressful.

Panel interviews are common in public sector appointments. The reason is that public sector recruitment is subject to considerable scrutiny to check that it is fair and open. This is clearly easier if more than one person is involved in the interview process. Sadly, sometimes panels of up to 15 people form for certain interviews, which makes life very difficult for the candidate trying to establish a good relationship with the recruiter.

The most important thing is to treat each question one at a time and listen carefully. Also, try to work out who are the key decision-makers or influencers on the panel, and try to concentrate on their concerns. With panels it's a good idea to tune in to the kind of language being used – is it abstract or concrete? Does the panel expect you to use certain buzz-words?

Interview Sequences

Be aware that some organizations will require you to go through two, three or even four interviews before a final selection decision is made. Find out how the decision will be made. Will you have to undergo further interviews? Don't suggest the idea, simply ask the open question *'May I just check when the final decision will be made, and who will be making it?'*. You may also be required to undertake ability or personality testing, or to participate in other forms of assessment (e.g. an in-tray exercise where you have to prioritize or comprehend a set of documents, or a group exercise where you are observed in a meeting or dealing with a team problem). These additional forms of assessment often worry candidates considerably. If you need to know more, these assessment measures are covered by a wide range of guides. However, anyone in recruitment will tell you that the stage that still matters most of all is the interview.

Interviewers – the Range of People You May Encounter

Attentive but Vague

This kind of interviewer listens responsively and asks some good questions, but isn't really in tune with the requirements of the job. This may be a first interview, and you'll meet the real decision-maker later. Or it could be that the organization itself is pretty vague about the position. Find out what you can, and concentrate on establishing a good relationship – this person could block your progress to a more productive stage.

Burned Out

This interviewer is well trained and highly experienced, but has seen better days. They may share inappropriate information with candidates (*'I don't know why anyone would want to work here ...'*). They may give a stress interview because this is what gets them through the day, and they will almost certainly demonstrate a lack of interest in your answers. Again, if this is a gatekeeper, do your best to be helpful and informative. If this is the final decision-maker and a key player in the organization, perhaps you ought to review a job offer carefully. Maybe this interview is telling you something useful about the company culture.

Inexperienced

This interviewer may be new to the field or new to the company. A very experienced job applicant must be careful to avoid patronizing this type of interviewer or demonstrating frustration for any reason. Don't embarrass the interviewer by appearing to know more about the company than he or she does – you will simply be marked down as arrogant, and this may be enough to prevent you moving further.

An inexperienced interviewer may not always ask the best questions. This shouldn't worry you if you are prepared. Don't ask for the questions to be rephrased, but jump right in with your job-related evidence.

Incompetent

Incompetent interviewers present you with a problem. They control access to the organization, and you're dependent on them to move you to the next stage. You may have only a vague sense of what will happen or where the interview is going. Questions may jump from topic to topic. Your main concern, however, is that the interviewer may be so focused on getting questions out that your answers are really not being heard. You may need to work hard to get your key message across. Summarizing your position is a fairly good idea.

Unprepared or Distracted

It's not at all uncommon for candidates to complain that they have been interviewed by unprepared questioners who have clearly not had time to read their CV. Avoid making a big deal of the interviewer's lack of preparation. If you imply any criticism (e.g. *'If you'd read my CV, you would have seen ...'*) you'll end up alienating a person who is already over-stressed by the job. If it's clear that you need to spell things out from first principles, take the time to do so.

Interviewers should protect themselves from distractions such as phone calls and interruptions. Whatever you do, do not take the distractedness personally. Something outside the interview process may have just had an impact on the interviewer, something you are powerless to do anything about. You can move the interview along the right track by refocusing on the key issues:

'Since you asked about my management experience, I would like to point out that, in addition to being in charge of my unit for the past three years, I have also taught classes in management at _____ University.'

Demanding, Prepared Professionals

This is the interviewer for whom you have prepared and with whom you hope to meet. However truly great interviewers are the exception rather than the rule. It is a really memorable experience to meet one of these individuals, regardless of the outcome. You will find that the interview is a challenging but really probing conversation. You depart feeling that you had an opportunity to provide a complete picture to the interviewer of who you are – and you may even have discovered something new about yourself in the process – you take away information about yourself that you had either forgotten or were never aware of.

When you plan for any interview, prepare and be ready to meet with this kind of interviewer. If they are prepared, they expect you to be as well.

Sharpen Your Interview Skill Set

Performing well at interview is a skill set like any other. Start working on your skills, and take them seriously.

Think about the range of skills you'll be using during the course of a job interview:

- Organizing information and resources.
- Reading people and situations.
- Listening attentively.
- Communicating complex information.
- Presenting ideas and information.
- Summarizing and synthesizing your experience.
- Speaking in an interesting and memorable way.

Don't use live interviews as the only way of improving your skills – take as many opportunities as you can to practise your techniques, undertaking interviews with work colleagues, those with management and interview experience, and also with recruitment consultants. At the same time, build up your job search skills (see **Chapter 3**).

The Changing Job Market

It's easy to find people who will say to you 'this is a really bad time to be changing jobs'. The interesting thing is that people say this in any job market – recession or otherwise. The reality is that the European and UK job market in the early part of the twenty-first century has been complicated. The decline of traditional manufacturing continues, while the rapid growth of the service sector we saw in the 1980s and 1990s shifted gear: Europe is continuing to develop added-valued service sector jobs (i.e. the 'knowledge economy' where specialist expertise or access to information is prized). On the other hand, a great deal of low-level service work (e.g. call centres and data processing) has been outsourced to overseas markets.

The UK and other European markets have seen both lay-offs and growth, long-term unemployment and skills short-ages. There is a national shortage of highly skilled manual workers – notably carpenters, plumbers and industrial cladders. Even traditional industries are becoming concerned about the difficulties of replacing experienced workers who are currently approaching retirement.

The press is full of news of redundancies, but the UK in particular has maintained record employment levels. Other factors include the rise of the 'greying population' – the proportion of the population of retirement age increases year by year.

This complex market brings opportunities and difficulties. At the beginning of the twentieth century Europe's two biggest sources of employment were domestic service and agriculture. A second factor is the rise of the career changer. Few employers look after the careers of their employees like the paternalistic organizations of a generation ago. Today's market is characterized by rapid shifts of the working population from one type of work to another, by frequent 'downsizing' and restructuring. If employers are no longer responsible for planning your career, who is? The answer is clear from the increasing number of people who are taking control of their own careers. Taking control is also about communicating the best of yourself at interview.

A Buyer's Market?

Let's investigate some of the blocks that prevent people getting anywhere near a job interview: the job myths that limit your job search activity.

You'll hear it said: '**There are a million applicants out there. It's a buyer's market.**' The media tends to give far more emphasis to the difficulties of redundant workers and the number of companies who are downsizing. You'll hear that employers aren't hiring at the moment, or they are putting job decisions on hold.

Human Resource professionals will tell you that if you run an ad for any position, you will be deluged with CVs by email, post and phone. CVs will come in from both applicants (suitable and unsuitable) and agencies. They have become a form of junk mail. With the proliferation of the personal computer and high-level word processing packages, it has become easier than ever to generate a well-presented and customized CV, and easier still to email the CV to any potential employer.

You will also hear employers say that they receive as many as 400 applications for published job advertisements. In addition, newspapers complain about a reduction in newspaper advertising.

All these factors are true, but they are only part of the picture. The bigger picture is this: people are getting jobs. In the UK, the downturn in job advertising after the attacks on the USA in September 2001 was not matched by an increase in unemployment. People are getting jobs, but they are doing so using different methods. The hidden job market has grown.

How Jobs Are Filled

In the not too distant past, technology was limited, mobility was less, and sources of information were fewer and harder to access than now. Job seekers could focus on what was close by and obvious. Your choices were limited and therefore you had a clearer idea of what was most relevant to pursue. Friends, relatives and neighbours all helped to identify opportunities in a narrow band of opportunity.

Now jobs are advertised in a huge variety of media, both print and online. The range of printed journals and newspapers carrying jobs has grown. Online vacancies are found on job boards, in listings maintained by recruitment agencies, and also on companies' own websites. A proportion of jobs are filled by recruitment agencies. And, more than ever it seems, a huge number of jobs are filled by word of mouth.

Chapter 2 will outline a number of strategies for job search success. For the moment, we need to pay attention to ways of increasing your chances of getting a job interview by understanding how jobs are filled. Understanding the ways employers prefer to fill positions provides some enormous insights into the kind of job search strategies that will create what you are looking for – an opportunity for a job interview.

The **Employers' Recruitment Methods** table on the following pages tells you more about the way organizations identify candidates, and spells out the advantages and disadvantages of various methods.

Employers' Recruitment Methods

How employers recruit	Why employers like or dislike this method	Advantages to applicant	Disadvantages to applicant
Internally advertised vacancy	Encourages career development, and candidates are already well known to the employer.	Limited pool of applicants. Your track record is already clear.	Unknown to applicant if not already employed there.
Recruiters, agencies	Screening done before candidates are referred. Agencies are often able to identify good candidates even at times of skill shortage.	You get some early feedback on your CV and interview technique.	Additional screening levels, potential delays. Agencies often screen out candidates who are not an obvious match.
Company-run Internet job board	Economical, and vacancies can be put up quickly. May not be seen by many external candidates.	Speed of access and submission. Vacancies may not be identified widely.	You may be up against internal applicants. You are an unknown quantity.
General Internet job boards	Again, very economical, but often result in an undifferentiated rush of CVs.	Speed of access and submission. You can use key words and phrases to be noticed.	You could be up against hundreds of hopefuls. Also, you have little control over the way your personal information is processed or sorted.

Newspaper or magazine advertisements	Present a professional image of the job and company and will reach the right people. Expensive.	One-stop source, and gives you plenty of clues about the job and the organization.	Will generate a large response.
Website or circulation list run by professional associations	Reaches the right calibre of candidate.	If you receive the listing, you're already considered suitable.	Limited to certain groups, and you may miss the vacancy if you don't keep up to date.
Careers services, Jobcentres	Low cost, but may not identify candidates with the right skills or qualities.	You will be assisted by an adviser, and at some skill levels there may not be many candidates presenting themselves.	Most jobs are entry level. You may not be given a great deal of information about the needs of the employer before interview.
Radio/TV	Expensive, and takes a long time from idea to production. Wide reach.	Urgency.	Again, will generate a large volume of undifferentiated applications. Will contain only limited details of the job.
Hiring someone connected to the organization	Contractors, consultants, temps. The advantage is that these candidates are a known quantity.	Great if you're already there, because your job-related evidence is first hand.	Difficult to get seen if you are not one of this 'inside' group.

Cont'd

Employers' Recruitment Methods (Cont'd)

How employers recruit	Why employers like or dislike this method	Advantages to applicant	Disadvantages to applicant
Word of mouth referral	Employers' preferred method. The perceived risk is lower where someone is referred to the organization by a staff member or trusted contact.	You can end up in a short list of one.	It's easy to get 'bounced' into an unsuitable job after getting an interview by this method. Check out the job and the organization as carefully as you would if you received a job offer by any other method.

Top 10 'Start-up' Tips

1. **Begin by browsing** through the book. Pick out the questions you know are most relevant to you, and the questions you will find it most difficult to answer. Start preparing your response.
2. **Plan your time** and use it effectively, particularly if you are unemployed. Make sure you take every opportunity to have regular meetings with peers and colleagues. Attend professional groups.
3. **Start working** with those areas in the book you are the strongest in. Ask colleagues with recruitment experience to practise interviews with you.
4. **Explore.** In casual conversations, ask what others like/dislike about their jobs. See what answers intrigue you.
5. **Take notes.** Write in the book. Do the worksheets.
6. **Maintain your friendships and contacts**. Looking for a job is hard work, and you will come across better in your interviews if you are not crushed under the weight of your search.
7. **Prepare yourself mentally.** Focus on your strengths. Do not get stuck criticizing yourself, but examine your behaviours and accentuate the positives.
8. **Enjoy the interview process** – meeting people, learning about different organizations. Be balanced: do other things as well as job search.
9. **Learn from each interview.** Whether you were offered the job or not, use each interview experience as a laboratory to develop better techniques and better answers.
10. **Prepare for rejection.** You'll get knock-backs – everyone does. Accept the fact that a proportion of interviews may be unsuccessful. Pick yourself up, cheer yourself up – but don't commit to a major change of strategy when you are at your lowest ebb.

2   What Are You Looking For?

KNOWING ENOUGH ABOUT
YOURSELF AND ABOUT
THE EMPLOYER

What job are *you* looking for? This is one of the first questions you should ask yourself before sending out any CVs and certainly before going on any interviews. What exactly do you want from a job? Have you worked out what you would really like to get out of a job – what is desirable, and what is essential? If those who do not study history are condemned to repeat it, then a wise move is to analyse your work history. Much of the time preparing for interviews and undergoing interviews revolves around self-analysis. So let's get started.

Looking at your current CV, what did you like about your past jobs? Using the **Job History Worksheet** (page 20), list your current and past jobs and what you liked and did not like about each job. Some of the likes and dislikes may be inherent in the job itself and are probably found in any organization, but others may change with the territory.

What did you learn from the list? Keep those likes and dislikes in mind as we turn from the past into the future.

What kind of an organization do you want to work for? Of the thousands of businesses out there, many will suit your individual needs. The trick is to recognize what you want in your next job. Do you like working for a big company or small? Do you prefer structured or free-flowing reporting? The exercise **My Ideal Job** (pages 20–21) helps you focus on your preferences.

Job History Worksheet

Jobs I have done:	Likes: The best parts of the job	Dislikes: the worst parts of the job
Organizational structure		
Company culture		
Management style		
Colleagues		
Products or services offered		
Skills I used		
Learning opportunities		
Opportunities to manage/supervise/ train others		
Other factors		

My Ideal Job

Circle your preferences and/or write in your own

The organization will be	small/large.
It will be in	a large city/a small town/the suburbs.
It should be within	_____ miles of my home.
It will be in the business of	service/products.

The business will be	a start-up/well established.
The business will be	publicly owned/private/government/not-for-profit.
The organization will be	conservative/avant-garde.
My position will require supervising others	a lot/somewhat/not at all.
I would like to work	on a team all the time/with others sometimes/alone most of the time.
I want to be supervised	closely/intermittently/from a distance.
I want to work with the public	all the time/from time to time/seldom.
My job should be	high tech/low tech/no tech.
I prefer to work with	people/things/data/ideas.
I prefer to work	on the phone/face-to-face/both.
I prefer to	delegate/do it myself.
My new job should be	same as old/different.
My work pace should be	slow/steady/busy or fast.
I want to be paid	a salary/commissions.
I want to travel	a lot/sometimes/never.
I want to work	in a big office/in a small office/in my own office/at home.
My weekly schedule should be	40 hours+/20–30 hours/part time/flexible.
I am available	for overtime/weekends.

Additionally, although salary is extremely important, often all those additional benefits can make or break a job offer. What are your basic requirements? Is on-site child care or flexitime a necessity? Which is more important to you, a pension or medical insurance? How important is a company car? What other benefits would you add to a wish list? Use the **New Job Wish List** below to list your focused requirements.

New Job Wish List

Deal makers	Deal sweeteners
List those elements that you feel you must have in any new job	List any perks/benefits that it would be nice to have

Include tangible benefits (e.g. salary, benefits, perks, time flexibility) and intangible benefits (e.g. learning opportunities, responsibility, the chance to exercise or develop particular skills)

What Kind of Work?

One of the decisions you need to make is about the nature of the work you are seeking, and the working hours you would like to do. You may need to be clear about this during an interview, and your decision will also have a big impact on you and the balance between work, home life, leisure, and study. Ring the options in the **Work Choices** opposite that appeal to you most.

Work Choices		
Full-time paid employment	Self-employment	Job Sharing
Part-time paid employment	Freelance	Temporary work
Full-time paid employment plus study	Consultancy	Casual work
Part-time paid employment for more than one employer	Interim management	Seasonal work
Part-time paid employment plus study	Semi-retirement	Voluntary work

What Do You Have to Offer?

Now it's time to complete a personal audit to get a sense of what you have to offer. This is a vital part of your 'message', and the principal reason why an employer will make time to bring you in for an interview.

Complete the **Personal Worksheet** (pages 24–25) next to look at all the things that make you distinctive. The last sections of the form ask you to look at what you really like to do and why. If you really like to programme computers but are looking for a position as a supervisor, this is time for a reality check. Perhaps supervisor positions pay more, or maybe there is a glut of programmers in the area. But if you love programming because of the detailed hands-on work and creativity, will you also love supervising programmers? Can you 'sell' yourself as a supervisor? Your financial needs are legitimate reasons for taking 'less than perfect' jobs as long as you are honest with yourself about your motivations.

Personal Worksheet

What I am Like: List all the adjectives that can be used to describe you. Some examples are given but add your own.

Aggressive	Calm	Cheerful	Co-operative
Creative	Dependable	Efficient	Flexible
Generous	Hardworking	Loyal	Methodical
Objective	Patient	Perceptive	Punctual
Sensitive	Terse	Uninhibited	Vibrant

What I can do: Examples are given but add your own.

Administer	Advise	Analyse	Budget
Calculate	Campaign	Co-ordinate	Delegate
Design	Evaluate	Identify	Initiate
Lead	Motivate	Negotiate	Plan
Prioritize	Problem solve	Summarize	Train

What I know: List everything that you know about, either through work or school or outside interests. Some examples are given but add your own.

Accounting	Art	Bookkeeping	Benefits
Computers	Economics	Electronics	Editing
Finance	Geography	Graphics	Healthcare
History	Language	Literature	Music
Programming	Repair	Selling	Writing

What I really like to do: Of all the things that you know and that you can do, list, in order of preference, the top 10 things you would like to do in your new job.

1. _____

2. _____

3. _____

4. _____

5. _____

6 _____

7. _____

8. _____

9. _____

10. _____

Why? List the reasons why you picked the top five preferences.

1. _____

2. _____

3. _____

4. _____

5. _____

Skills

When completing the **Job History Worksheet** (page 20) you may have come across some difficulty recording your skills. Many job changers only see half the picture when it comes to their own skill set, because they only see (a) the skills that others recognize and value and (b) the skills that seem to be valuable to organizations.

Look in detail at the skills you have required for each job you have done. Which skills do you use with a high level of competence? What skills do you have that others don't?

Most importantly of all, think about the **evidence** that you have to support any statement you might have about skills. Evidence might include:

- Qualifications.
- Certificates of attendance on training courses.
- Company reports.
- Written praise from managers or customers.
- Appraisal records.
- Awards or prizes.
- A portfolio recording work you have performed.
- Photographs, models, prototypes, press cuttings.

It's worth writing out your job history afresh, looking at each job as a series of problems. What situations or problems did you have to address? What skills did you use? What outcomes did you achieve?

As you record them, write them down in the **Skills Inventory** below.

Skills Inventory

Skills associated with INFORMATION	Skills associated with IDEAS
Skills associated with THINGS	Skills associated with PEOPLE

Think about whether you use these skills in a high or low order way, e.g.:

Low order/simple skills	Comparative high order/ complex skills
Counting	Analysing
Making	Designing
Instructing	Coaching/mentoring
Working to plans	Project management
Transacting	Negotiating

By definition, the higher the skills you exercise, the more freedom you have to exercise them in the way you wish.

Your Target Job

Now, drawing information together, you may find it helpful to write a description of your target job and ideal organization, as shown in the following example.

My ideal job will be in a small, family-run company in my home town. I would like a high tech, innovative company, and one which is small enough for me to have some real impact on commercial decisions and strategy. Although I want a short commute to work I am happy to travel in my job. I would love to have my own office but it's not vital, although I dislike big open-plan offices.

I want to be part of a close-knit team of equals who give each other a great deal of support. I want a manager who's more of a coach than a supervisor.

Position: Supervise 10–15 programmers, make own departmental recruitment decisions and control a budget. Salary £xxx, or the ability to reach that within 12 months.

This is your 'wish list' to refer to throughout your job search. Notice that it is written on paper, not in stone. Make adjustments as needed.

Give some preliminary thought to the availability of such jobs (how are you going to find them?) and also determine what pay level you need.

Reality Check

As stated elsewhere, it is not necessarily the best candidate who gets the job, but usually the best interviewee. Make that the best *informed* interviewee. Go to the library and look up any information available about your target organization. You can find reference books and directories in most large libraries, but you will find that a huge amount of information about companies is now available on the Internet. Try looking, in addition, at periodicals and industry publications.

- What types of organizations are you applying to?
- Are they private companies or PLCs?
- What is their main product or service?
- How long have they been in business?
- What exactly is their business?
- How many employees are on-site?
- Who are their competitors?
- How big are they?
- How has business been lately?
- How do they conduct their business?
- What major trends or problems might affect them?

If appropriate, call up the organization and request a recent annual report or any other publications. Use the **Organization Fact Sheet** (pages 29–30) to gather facts about the organization. You can create a 'file' by attaching any articles or additional information regarding the organization or the industry. Other questions are:

- How did I learn of this job opening?
- How long has the job been open?
- What is the job description?
- What about salary and benefits?

Now, look at your 'ideal' organization on your index card. How close are you? Do you have enough information? What additional information do you need? On the **Need to Know List** (page 31) record all the information to be gathered prior to your interview, or questions to ask at the interview itself. As you get additional information, add it to your file or **Organization Fact Sheet**. By the time you go to the interview, your remaining questions either won't be important or they can be answered in the interview itself. You may also want to hold back some questions until you get a job offer. **Chapter 14** discusses this in greater depth.

Organization Fact Sheet

1 The Organization

Name of organization:

Address:

Telephone:

Contact person:

Names of people interviewing:

Title: Telephone number:

Email:

Office location:

Referred by:

Nature of business:

How many years trading:

Number of employees:

Number of locations/sites:

Ownership:

Senior management:

Recent sales/earnings:

What has been trend past five years?

Markets:

Market share:

Leading competitors:

Trends/recent developments:

Other information:

2 The Position

Job title:

Where advertised:

Name and contact details of recruitment consultant:

Job description:

   Main tasks

   Major responsibilities

   Key result areas

Size of unit:

Location of unit:

Reports to:

Salary range:

Other information:

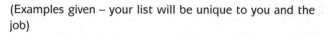

Need to Know List

(Examples given – your list will be unique to you and the job)

How long has the position been open?

How many on the short list?

When will the final decision be made?

Are accounts published? How is the company doing compared to others in its sector?

Does marketing report directly to the MD? If not, to whom?

Size of department's annual budget/staffing requirements?

Organization chart: others on 'my' level?

How is the department viewed by senior management? Do they like current ad campaigns or are they planning to outsource in future? What per cent is spent annually in various media?

Top 10 Tips for Job Hunting

1 Be **proactive**, not passive. Decide what you want to do, and make a career decision around clear goals rather than the first job to come along.
2 Work out your **wish list**: the skills you want to use, the environment you want to work in, the kind of problems you want to deal with.
3 Compose a clear **message** to employers: what you have to offer, and what you are looking for. Your message is in everything you do and say. Make it clear and positive.
4 Don't accept **limitations** imposed on you by others. Focus on what you can do, and where you have succeeded.

5 Have **confidence** in yourself and your abilities. Employers buy confidence as much as experience.

6 Use a **multi-strategy** job search including direct speculative applications, job boards, recruitment consultants and networking.

7 Think about what motivates you in work. What inspires you to get out of bed and go to work?

8 What kind of work have you **chosen** to do, either in your leisure time or as a volunteer? Often the work we *choose* to do without financial constraint is a great clue to our best work.

9 Look at the **skills** you *really* enjoy using, when you are impossible to distract and rarely bored. Do you prefer to work mainly with things, concepts, information or people?

10 Think **research before job search**. Talk to people about the jobs they do. Learn from the mistakes others have made.

Analysing and Communicating Your Skills

For more on discovering your skills, see John Lees' *How To Get A Job You'll Love* (McGraw-Hill). You may also find the **JLA Skill Card Sort** useful – a tool designed to spot your primary skills and show you how to communicate them to decision-makers.

The Skill Cards come with a full set of instructions to assist career changers, and the exercise provides a useful source of achievement evidence for job interviews.

See **www.johnleescareers.com** for further details.

3

Winning Your Way to the Interview

YOUR FIRST STEP

Where and How to Find Jobs

If one of the greatest challenges for employers is to find suitable candidates, *your greatest challenge is to find employers who are ready and willing to offer you a job interview.*

In spite of downsizing, the UK continues to have a vibrant and resilient economy. Not every sector is going through the same part of the activity cycle. While new industries are going through periods of explosive growth, others are in their maturity stage, and still others are in a period of decline. Some occupations stay in decline while stock markets are depressed, particularly IT stocks. Other sectors, e.g. the health sector, continue to expand. Chambers of Commerce commonly say they don't know how many businesses are in operation at any one time, because at the precise moment some businesses are opening their doors for the first time, other are closing theirs. A large proportion of new businesses are small and medium enterprises (SMEs) – a fact that should convince you that the traditional methods of finding a job (searching the job advertisements and registering with just one or two agencies) are even less likely to succeed in the future.

The other key thing to realize is that thousands of *new kinds of jobs* are being created every year – not just vacancies but jobs that didn't exist before. Keep up to date, and keep asking questions which will lead you to the right organizations.

Some of the key questions you should be asking yourself and others about your target job market are covered below in the exercise **Questions to Begin Your Job Search**. If you don't have the answers, you have a good reason to start asking questions.

Questions to Begin Your Job Search
Who are the largest employers in my sector?
Which of them are in my travel to work area?
Who is growing?
Who has won new contracts recently?
Who has won a business award recently?
How do my target companies recruit?
Where do they advertise?
Who is advertising for staff regularly?
Who uses its own website for advertising vacancies?
Who has recently moved to the area?
Who has been laying staff off (and maybe got rid of the wrong people)?
Who do I know who knows someone who works in, supplies or deals with any of these companies?

How to Get Started

The key thing is to make sure that you have a clear message in everything you use to communicate your 'offer'. Your message includes everything written about you (CV, application form, covering letter, online application) but also includes everything you say about yourself in informal and formal situations:

Informally when contacts are asking about the kind of work you'd like to do. This may happen when you are networking, talking to former colleagues, or in a wide variety of social situations.

Formally when you are in front of a decision-maker in an interview situation.

In all contexts what works well is having a **clear, positive message** – a 'wish list' of the kinds of things you would like to do. Working through the checklists in this book will help you to define what that wish list contains.

The Work Your CV Has To Do For You

It is so hard to be considered for any job because, once an ad is placed, the organization is flooded with CVs. The problem is getting your CV noticed and picked from all the others received. **Your CV must rise to the top on the wave of paper submitted**. It is just not enough to assume your CV sparkles because of your specific relevant experience. It needs to have visibility and be separated from all the others. This requires a timely arrival, a visually attractive document, and dependence on the person screening the CV to be able to identify that particularly relevant experience.

There are many do's and don'ts regarding CVs and job applications (see *How To Get A Job You'll Love* by John Lees for a full set of checklists). Perhaps the critical piece of advice is this: **make your message match the job**.

There is a simple technique for this. Take an A4 piece of paper and rule a line down the middle. On the left-hand side write down all the information you can about the job and the organization. Write down everything you can find from the job ad, the job description, and any other documents available to you. Include any extra information you have discovered through informal approaches. Then take a high-light pen and mark the key criteria that you think the short-listing staff will be using. Transfer these to the **Employer Requirements Checklist** (below) and on the right-hand side try to fill in how you match up to each one.

Employer Requirements Checklist

Anticipated top 10 requirements of the employer	My matching evidence

---

When you have completed the **Employer Requirements Checklist** look for the gaps. You may find that you don't have enough insights yet to help you understand exactly what the organization is looking for. If this is the case, you will find it useful to use the **Organization Fact Sheet** on pages 29–30. It's equally likely that you won't yet have all the facts you need to complete the 'evidence' column of the checklist. You'll find a great many prompts on this score throughout this book, and you'll also find that many of the questions covered here are good prompts to help you think about your matching experience, strengths and know-how.

One quick tip: if you find there are key requirements and you don't have particularly strong matching evidence, don't give up. The important thing to remember is that if you ignore a key requirement, your application is fairly likely to end up on the 'no' or 'maybe' pile. You may keep your fingers crossed that the recruiter will ignore your 'gap', but this is unlikely. After all, if the requirement is important, then it's important enough to use to short-list. Your best strategy is to provide evidence for your matching strengths, and then to refer specifically to any area where you can show parallel rather than exactly matching experience. Your application letter might say, for example:

'Your advertisement asks for a Chartered Marketeer. While I am not yet professionally qualified in this field, I have attended a number of training courses at professional level. In addition, I believe that my 10 years' experience in this field gives me the right experience and background to succeed in this post.'

Reading Job Ads Creatively

If you are going to stick to job ads, there's more than one way of reading them. Look at each advertisement from these four different angles:

1. Is this the right **job** for me? If so, what do I need to do to win an interview?
2. Is this the right **company** for me? Who do I write to if I want to offer my services for a role which hasn't been advertised (yet)?
3. Is this the right **field of work** for me? What are this company's main competitors?
4. Is there a **recruitment consultant** handling this position? If so, they may have other jobs coming on stream soon.

Avoid the Numbers Game

Most job-seekers rely on passive methods of job-seeking as outlined below.

Passive Methods Much Beloved By Job-seekers

Responding to published vacancies in newspapers.

Registering with online job boards.

Registering with recruitment consultancies.

The problem with the passive method is that you rely on other people to make a decision. Also, you play very long odds. If 300 people apply to a newspaper advertisement, your chances of being short-listed for an interview list of, say, six people are pretty poor, **no matter how good your CV and your experience.**

Therefore it makes sense also to look at more **active** methods of generating interviews:

Active Methods Rarely Used By Job-seekers

Applying directly to companies. This works best if your letter is targeted carefully to the key decision-maker, by name. Your letter should say something about the organization's anticipated needs, not just things about you.

Building a relationship with an organization who create a job for you. This happens far more often than you think. Once an organization gets to know you, they may feel they can't live without you. But building this relationship takes time – and is often built up through short-term or consultancy work.

Networking your way to an interview. Employers prefer to hire people they already know, or people who are known to someone close at hand.

> **Support your written application with a personal approach**. This isn't about lobbying for the job, but about establishing personal contact with a recruiter to reinforce your application. If the job ad invites you to ring up to discuss a position, do so. If the position is being handled by a recruiter, try to have a conversation. In both cases, make sure you have some detailed, job-related questions to ask so your call can't be blocked by an administrator.

Build Active Relationships With Recruitment Consultants

These people are relationship-driven. Getting just one or two of them on your side can make a big difference. One way to use them well is to understand how they can help you to get the job.

Questions to Ask Recruitment Consultants

Meetings with recruiters and agencies are screening interviews. The interviewers, if satisfied that you are a possible fit, refer you to the organization directly for an interview. The organization (the client) is given either a copy of your CV or a synopsis of your experience and qualifications prepared by the agency.

Don't forget that an agency doesn't make the final decision, but performs a short-listing service. Agencies look for people who are a strong match to an employer's requirements, but also people who interview well. A recruiter can't give you all the inside information about a job, but can usually tell you the key issues.

Questions to Put to a Recruitment Consultant Before Going to an Employer

Is there a detailed job description?

What are the key result areas of the job?

To whom does the position report?

Why is the position open?

What happened to the last post holder?

How long has the position been open?

How long have you had the assignment?

What's the likely pay range?

Who will be interviewing me? Who is the decision-maker?

What's the company culture?

What dress code would you advise?

What kind of people do well in this organization?

Who will make the final selection decision?

Are there any other written materials to review before I agree to a meeting?

The Power of Referrals

A high proportion of job openings come from referrals. Why? Because employers behave like anyone else, and prefer to commit to people with whom they have a relationship. Would you give your house keys to a stranger or to a neighbour? Would you make a high-value purchase from someone you had met 10 minutes ago? In the same way, you're asking an employer to make a high-value commitment, and the employer will be far more comfortable doing that if he or she feels they know you.

This is the power of **networking** – a word that often puts people off. It's not about the 'old school tie' or about gaining an unfair advantage. It's about finding people who can help you to get close enough to decision-makers so they will feel comfortable meeting you. In other words, about *generating meetings*.

Make things happen for yourself. Get out and interact with people who can make connections for you. Take a class, read books, get out and network with others in your profession, go to the library and do research, contact professional organizations to find out about meetings and membership. Talk to others at meetings – just to discover information and to get yourself known. With the possible exception of stressful job interviews, people love to talk about themselves – particularly if they are in a job they love doing.

Actively recruit people to be on your side. The more people who know that you are actively searching for a new job, the more chances you have to get lines on future interviews. **Follow the 'arm's-length' rule: Everyone within arm's-length of you should know you are looking for a job.** You never know who may overhear your conversation while standing in the supermarket queue, waiting for a train or a plane, or someone standing next to you reading the job ads in the newspaper.

Remember – it's far more productive to chase opportunities for meetings with organizations than it is to chase job openings.

5 Steps to Successful Networking

STEP 1 – COMPILE A TARGET LIST
Write a list of all the people who may be able to help you – with practice interviews, with information about different careers, with inside information about organizations, and also about job openings. Don't just think of relatives and friends, but all contacts, no matter how loose the connection.

STEP 2 – DEFINE YOUR AIMS
Define and write down the areas you want to research. What fields of work do you want to know more about? What organizations would you like to talk to? What background information do you need to be able to 'talk the talk' at an interview? Make a note of the specific questions to which you seek answers.

STEP 3 – MAKE CONTACT
It's always easier to get a meeting through someone you already know. Telephone is the best method of initial contact, but letters sometimes work – particularly if your letter is interesting and focuses on the needs of the company rather than yourself.

Ask for a meeting of 20–30 minutes (you are likely to get longer, but 20–30 minutes is easier for busy executives to accommodate within their schedules and does not indicate any pressure). Offering two alternative dates/times can help your contact to agree a meeting.

If your contact wants to deal with you quickly on the telephone, it's a good idea to say that you always find face-to-face meetings more useful because it gives you a chance to get a feel for the organization. It certainly does – you gain about 200% more information from a face-to-face meeting than you do from a telephone conversation, *and* you're remembered for a lot longer.

If you can't find anyone close by, use the telephone bounce back technique. You might speak to someone who is inconveniently at the other end of the country. Ask if they can suggest somebody closer to your home town who is in a similar field.

Remember, however the conversation goes, it's always worth asking the question *"Who else should I be talking to?"*.

STEP 4 – TIME MANAGEMENT

Plan a networking meeting just as you would any other important business discussion. Don't be over-formal with an agenda, but have some clear objectives in your mind before you start, and a note of the main questions you want to ask.

Try to schedule your meetings to avoid travelling to the same town on successive days, or having two meetings in the same area but at each end of the day, with nothing planned for in-between.

STEP 5 – EFFECTIVE MEETINGS

Use your plan carefully, and make the most of the valuable time you have with any contacts. Be very clear about what you are asking them. If you are asking for news of vacancies, say so. If you're simply finding out more about a particular industry sector, make that clear. But always ask contacts to do something that you believe is within their power – networking contacts are always happier if they can be helpful.

Try to avoid asking obvious questions that you could answer for yourself with a little homework. Focus on the things that are going to be really useful to you in future interviews: the way the industry is going, who are the movers and shakers, what kind of people are being hired, and what kind of experience is valued? If your contact tells you about minimum qualifications, find out whether there is any way into your chosen occupations without them.

At minimum, try to use each networking meeting, to obtain the names of at least two other contacts who can help your continued research.

Be Prepared For Delays and Setbacks

There are times when the economy lacks certainty, and during these times employers sometimes demonstrate frustrating behaviours. They give out messages such as '*The position is put on hold.*' '*We are rethinking our strategy … reorganizing … eliminating the department … merging into a group function.*' This news can be disheartening, and can come up any time during the selection process and even just at the job offer point.

Fortunately this kind of setback is rare. What is much more common is that organizations take some time to come to a decision, and occasionally put decisions on hold. This is simply the way the market works, and it's important that you see it that way. The fact that an employer takes 2 months to respond to a letter is probably not a reflection of your abilities, but just says something about the organization. Equally, if an employer takes a long time to get back to you after an interview, don't always assume that the answer is 'no'. If an employer prevaricates or puts a decision on ice, it's often because the company as a whole is finding it hard to commit to the future at a time of uncertainty.

Key Points on Winning the Interview

- Your CV or application wins you the meeting, not the job. Don't oversupply information.
- Try to work out the employer's shopping list – the deal-breakers that will get you short-listed.
- Present (briefly, and in bullet point form) your matching evidence and strengths. Again, don't feel you have to say everything about yourself.
- Try not to offer any information which will get you excluded at this stage (e.g. detailed queries about salary, terms and conditions, pension entitlement, or hours of work).
- Don't rely purely on passive job search methods unless you believe in very long odds.
- Use as many active methods as possible to generate interviews.
- Whatever you send, give the interviewer at least three or four strong reasons to see you.

4

Preparation is the Key

PLANNING TO SUCCEED

The Interview Process

An interview is a conversation with a specific purpose. Both parties to the interview want something from the process. So the goal of the interview for both parties is to feel that they have achieved their goals. The greater the area of common goals met, the greater the probability of a job offer.

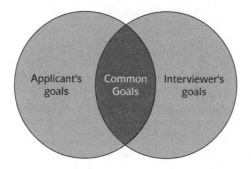

Realizing that both the interviewer and applicant have goals is important. If you don't allow the interviewer to achieve his or her goals, you'll create the impression of failure and you probably won't get a job offer. If you don't achieve your own goals you won't have come over at your best. If you achieve the crossover goals you get closer to a real win/win between yourself and the decision-maker, and ultimately between yourself and the organization.

The first step is to determine that both the interviewer and interviewee agree on the **purpose of the meeting**. Are you looking to fill a specific position? Is this position open? Do you meet the requirements of the position? Given the job description, are you interested in the position as it currently exists?

It's possible to break down any interview into a small number of key question areas, as set out below in **The 6-point structure at the heart of all interview questions**.

The 6-point Structure at the Heart of All interview Questions

1. What brought you to us? Why did you apply? What is your career plan?
2. What do you have to offer? What do you bring to the party? What solutions do you have to offer which match our problems?
3. How well do you understand us? Have you worked out how we tick as an organization? Have you worked out the key result areas of the job?
4. Who are you? What kind of person are you? Are you like us? Will you fit in? What will you add to a team?
5. Why you? – rather than someone else with the same general profile? What puts you ahead of the pack? What's your unique selling point?
6. What will it take to bring you on board? What will you cost us? How do we have to motivate and develop you to retain you in the future?

From *How To Get A Job You'll Love*, John Lees, McGraw-Hill 2003.

Who is the 'buyer' and who is the 'seller' in the interview? What is more important to you, do you hear the interviewer's message, and does the interviewer hear yours? What exactly do you want to get out of this interview? What do you want to 'give' the interviewer?

Interview Basics

1. What is the **purpose** of the interview?
2. What information do you want to **get** from the interview?
3. What information do you want to **give** at the interview?

Planning – The Essential Ingredient

After all your preparation, letter writing, CV mailings and telephone follow-ups, the day of the interview has arrived.

Don't make the mistake of the average job-seeker by believing that you can 'wing it' on the day. Most people take an essentially passive approach, believing '*I don't know what they'll ask me, so I will respond as things come up*'. The experiences of thousands of interviewees will tell you that this doesn't work. You will work hard in the interview itself, but you need to work harder before it happens.

Location and Travel

Call to confirm the place and time if it's not clear from the written instructions. It's a good idea to ring anyway to ask exactly where you have to be, and to check where you can park. If you are directed to a public car park, ask in advance whether you need change for a Pay and Display system.

Plan your route. Some candidates even do a 'dummy run' the day before if it's a really important interview. Make sure you allow plenty of time so that you have a big safety margin. Sitting quietly in the car park is fine, and arriving early is also usually acceptable, if not welcomed. Besides, arriving early may give you a chance to have a quick look around or talk to the reception staff.

The Interview Process Starts the Moment of Your Arrival

Once you enter the building, be alert and listen to what is going on around you. All your senses should be operating to evaluate this organization as one in which you may choose to spend most of your waking hours for years to come. Consider the overall appearance of the offices and the attitudes of the workers you meet.

If you can think of the interview as similar to a first date, then the meeting place should be evaluated in terms of the importance the employer places on these dates. Instead of parents meeting you at the door and giving you the once-over, every employee you come in contact with (particularly in the reception area) may be asked to give feedback about you to the decision-makers. This is a two-way street: you are also evaluating the organization through the actions and attitudes of the employees you meet.

Pre-interview Checklist

✓ **Name and title** of person you are meeting, with correct spelling and punctuation. If you think you'll have difficulty pronouncing the name right, ring in advance and check with reception.

✓ **Exact address** and location of the organization including directions to the office building, car parking instructions, and a map.

✓ **Research notes** regarding the organization and the position for you to review en route (an index card or two should suffice to capture main points).

✓ **List of points** you want to make.

✓ Some pre-prepared **questions** for the end of the interview.

✓ **Employment and educational** history in case you are asked to complete an application form. (See **Experience Worksheet, page 149.**)

✓ Your **business card** if you have one.

✓ A copy of the **job advertisement** and **job description**.
✓ A copy of the **CV** and letter you used to win the interview.
✓ While waiting, 'warm up' by passing small talk with others that you run across in the reception area or on the way to the interview.
✓ Size up the interview site. What status does the interviewer appear to have within the organization?
✓ Check out the attitudes of employees you may see. What do they say about the way this organization treats its staff?
✓ Switch off your **mobile phone** before entering the building. You don't need any distractions.

First Impressions

Make no bones about this issue. First impressions count.

Some research studies have suggested that interviewers make up their minds within the first 2 minutes of an interview. Even if the interviewer has not come to a final decision, even the most objective, well-trained interviewer has received some kind of formative impression from:

- What you look like (dress, smartness, appropriateness ...).
- How you move (confidently, hesitantly, clumsily ...).
- What you have with you (do you look prepared and professional?).
- How you sound (clear, confident, mumbling).

Keep the greeting simple. If a hand is offered, give a firm (dry) handshake. Even though some may not consider the interviewer's greeting and your response important, they are missing an important part of the meeting.

Don't be too formal or informal – use first names if invited to do so, and be willing to reciprocate.

You will be assessed by the speed in which you can establish a relationship, get comfortable, and start talking about yourself.

You may also be affected by first impressions. Don't tune out of the meeting because your first impression of the interviewer or the process is negative. Always be professional and see it through to its conclusion, but check out whether your experience is really reflective of the organizational culture – your interviewer may just be having a bad day.

The Interview Site

Since you have taken time to consider how you present (or sell) yourself, from packaging (your clothes, your CV) to content (the research and analysis that preceded the interview), it is only fair for you to evaluate how the organization presents itself. The interview location is the 'sales office.' Are they making any effort to 'sell' themselves to you as a prospective employer?

The interview site is a great opportunity for you to be a communication sponge. Consider what messages the meeting place sends about the importance that the organization places on the person you are meeting and the importance the organization places on the meeting itself.

Consider the meeting room and everything about it. What floor is it on? What other organizational units are located on the same floor? Then look around the room. Is there a door (for privacy)? Does the room have windows? A view? The furniture, fixtures and artwork or other items displayed on the walls set a tone. Does the room have time-sensitive material displayed? For example, it's November and there are notices for the company picnic, or some of the 'employee of the month' plaques are missing for several past months. What does this reveal about the organization and its occupants? Soak it all up. You need to learn as much as you can about what the organization wants to project as an image. You need to confirm in your own mind a consistency or inconsistency in their messages.

The Meeting Itself

This is why you are there. Be alert to all your surroundings and to the presentation of your interviewer. If you have received a letter with the interviewer's name and title in confirmation of your interview, be certain to use the person's name as soon as possible. Doing so helps you to remember it and to establish rapport.

Pay careful notice to the organization's use of time before, during and even after the meeting takes place. If an organization conducts interviews on time, and runs a well-organized schedule, it's usually a fair indication of standards. If 30 minutes pass before your scheduled meeting occurs, the delay might be just an unusual occurrence or it might be the organization's approach to time. What should you do? Is anyone aware of the fact that your appointed time has come and gone? Does the receptionist think this is no big deal? Sloppiness may be the result of staff shortages or things going wrong, but sometimes badly-planned interviews reflect a poor approach to the whole area of recruitment and employment practice.

Look also at the way the organization values the interview itself. Does the interviewer get interrupted by telephone calls? Was he or she asked to step out of the room? Was a closed door ignored? These, too, are clues about organizational culture. You can use such clues when you make a decision about whether you want to work there, but you can also draw upon such clues in deciding how you play the interview.

Q1 Tell me one thing you find stimulating about your present job.

Here's a starter. You could be faced with a detailed question like this relatively early on in the interview. Listen carefully to the questions, and get into a rhythm of concise, clear responses. Make your answers as clear as possible. Most interviewees say far too much, and interviewers 'tune out' fairly quickly if they are bored or over-supplied with information. Remember that many questions, particularly in the first part of the interview, are simply there to get you talking and to establish basic facts. Your interviewer will start to ask supplementary or probing questions if more information is required. Keeping initial answers concise makes them more effective:

'I find a number of things stimulating – it's a good team, and the work provides a number of challenges. What I really enjoy is the sense of achievement when I win new business.'

You Are What You Communicate

What is the relevance of the interview if oral communication is not a major job requirement? If you're trying to find a job you may resent the interview process because it seems to get in the way: *'I'm looking for a job, not to have interviews. Why can't they judge me by reviewing my paperwork and giving me a written test? I can do the job – why do I have to go through this rigmarole?'*

This frustration is inevitable, and you'll be particularly aware of it if you dislike interviews. However, get one thing clear in your mind: doing well at interview is the only way you'll get the job – whether communication skills are part of the job or not.

The reason is that interviewers have very little to go on outside the evidence they glean during an interview. They may have some test results, letters from referees, possibly also the results of some other form of assessment. However, what happens during the interview is critical, because it is during this time that an interviewer makes a series of decisions:

- Has this person performed these tasks well in the past?
- How will this person perform in the future?
- Will he/she fit in?
- Is this the right person for the job?
- What does this candidate have to offer that others don't?
- Is he/she going to be an asset or a problem?

Winning at interview is essentially about offering a clear, positive answer to all of these questions.

If you lack the ability to get your points across, you'll feel a deep sense of frustration about the interview process. You may be unable to communicate your work experience effectively even though you have been very successful in your work, possibly even an expert in your field. In short, communication is vital, even if it isn't in the job itself.

Hearing Versus Listening

Under stress, we listen even more ineffectively. Think of a time when you have been worried about something, and someone's talked to you about a trivial subject like the cost of photocopying paper. What small percentage of what you heard actually registered? How much more difficult can an interview be when so much is on the line?

Listening is a powerful tool if you're on the receiving end of an interview. It can provide you with vital clues – what do you say? How long should your answers be? Does the interviewer want to hear more? Preparing material in advance means that you are a much more effective listener – you can keep your 'radar' fully switched on during the interview rather than getting caught up in your inner turmoil of wondering what on earth you're going to say next. This is one of the main reasons you are encouraged to work out some developed **Presentation Statements** (see **Chapter 6**).

Tools for Effective Listening

- Relax as far as you can.
- Pay attention to your surroundings. Take in the way things look and sound around you.
- Listen carefully to the language the interviewer is using. Try to mirror its style (formal/informal, technical/non-technical, free-ranging or tightly focused).
- Learn to be an active listener. This means paying attention to the speaker and valuing what is said.
- Be aware of the listener's body language. Comfortable? Attentive? Eager to move on to another topic? Bored?
- Do not interrupt.
- Respond with empathy when the interviewer mentions a difficulty or problem facing the firm.
- Don't be afraid of silence. You are allowed time to think.
- Don't jump in and say the first thing that comes into your head.
- Prepare in advance for difficult questions (see **Chapter 12**).

The first step in becoming a better listener – an active listener – is to start right now. In all your conversations – with family, friends, 'small talk' with strangers – slow it down and start listening.

Learn to reflect as you speak. Quit worrying about coming up with snappy answers: it's fine to hesitate a moment to 'gather your thoughts' before answering. These pauses can be easily read as a sign of respect, an acknowledgement of the importance of the question. Take a quiet, calming breath. Unclench those hands and sit comfortably in the chair. Train your focus on the person who is speaking. Is he or she speaking fast or slowly? How much eye contact is there? Differences in style can create tension, but accepting differences can help you concentrate, which can lead to better understanding.

Do not label the speaker. Do not become so impressed that the interviewer is a 'giver of jobs' that this becomes a block to effective listening. Listen to everyone without prejudice as to the source of the information. What you do with the information can be decided later when you can 'consider the source'. Do not put up barriers to your listening.

Listen actively. Do not be afraid to ask questions to further the information being given. Show the speaker that you are listening by offering eye contact. Make slight gestures of affirmation (a smile, nodding the head, comments) to show that your attention is with the speaker. If you do not understand a point, ask that it be explained further or restate it, '... *in other words, you are looking for ...*'.

Do not assume anything. Do not jump to conclusions and begin an answer before the interviewer has set out the full terms of the question. Gather all the information available before offering a comment or solution. **Let the interviewer ask the question completely.** Jumping in too early can make speakers feel that they are doing a poor job of communicating because you just cannot wait to go where they are not heading!

Put yourself in the other person's shoes. What is the speaker looking for? What are the other person's needs? You can try to sway other persons' opinions or obtain influence only after you understand them. Look for issues or unsatisfied needs as 'buttons' to push. *You are offering yourself as a solution to someone else's problems*; you must listen closely to determine specifically what those problems are and how you can uniquely solve them.

Finally, be aware of the right **talking and listening balance.** Some say the more that job applicants can get interviewers to do the talking, the greater is the likelihood that they will be successful. People love to hear themselves talk. So it follows that, if interviewers get to do a lot of talking, they feel good about themselves. If they feel good about themselves, they credit the person who is responsible for this feeling.

Relationship Building

If it's true that interviewers make up their minds fairly early on in an interview, it's also true that a number make another subjectivity error: they hire people they like. This usually happens at a subconscious level, but – no matter how unfair – this reaction also has its usefulness. The interviewer is trying to work out an answer to the question 'How would I get on with this person as a colleague?'. If you get on during the interview, it's a reasonable assumption (though hardly scientific) that you will do so in future.

This means that one of your objectives is to make the interviewer feel comfortable. This may seem rather the reverse of what normally happens in interviews, but if you don't take some responsibility for building rapport, you're relying very heavily on the interviewer's skills. Look carefully at the things that interviewers say to help to build a relationship:

- The candidate responds openly to the interviewer's handshake, smile and opening remarks.
- The candidate seems to find the questions stimulating and interesting.
- The candidate listens and speaks carefully, respecting the interviewer's point of view and not interrupting.
- The interview candidate responds positively to probing questions and affirms when summaries are correct.
- The interviewer and interviewee discover that they have things in common.
- Both parties appear to share similar values.
- The candidate says a warm thank-you for the interview.

Taking the Edge Off Interviews – Key preparation points

- **Prepare** as thoroughly as you would if this was the only job offer you'll get this year.
- **Know** your strengths and weaknesses. Be prepared to talk about the way your personality fits into work (see also **Chapter 7**).
- Research the organization (see also **Chapter 2**).
- **Relate** your skills to the specific job opening.
- **Look** at your job history and education from a number of different angles. Anticipate probing questions.
- **Turn** things around. What questions would you ask yourself?
- Ask **SO WHAT**? about every line in your CV. Have you really communicated your strengths. Do you stand out from the crowd? If not, prepare more evidence.
- Face your fears. What questions are you terrified they will ask. Rehearse your answers.
- Sell yourself. **Tell** them exactly why they should appoint you.
- **Show** the value that you will add to the organization.
- **Allay their fears** (you won't perform, will take too long to come on stream, cause problems, be late/absent, not stay...).

5

Opening Questions

BREAKING THE ICE

As mentioned in the previous chapter, the opening of the interview is a critical stage. Interviews often begin with small talk. The first question put to you might be 'Isn't it a lovely day?'. Psychologists call this a *low order question* – in other words, a question that takes very little brain power to generate a response.

Interviews begin with small talk. Small talk makes social situations easier; it 'oils the wheels'. It is something that can be used (and perfected) in a variety of situations – personal and professional – and if used lightly and with humour is often a great technique for drawing people into conversation.

We live in an age when face-to-face communication skills are more important than ever, yet ironically there are many aspects of culture that discourage their development. Television, the Internet, email and computer games – these are all technological developments that dominate our lives and reduce the need for interactions with real people. The ability to initiate and maintain interesting conversations may be a dying art – but it's a vital tool in the interview process.

The Problem with Most Small Talk – You Need an Agenda

We have a natural 'agenda' for small talk. If we're in line at a supermarket checkout, for example, we say things about common experiences: the long wait, sale items, high prices, how busy or quiet the store is. We have all found ourselves in similar circumstances – stuck on long airplane flights, in delayed trains, in doctor or dentist offices – when chatting with others (or being chatted to) is one way to pass the time.

The tool is even more important when we want to establish some kind of a relationship with someone. We all know that if you're going to ask for a discount in a shop, you have a much better chance if you start with some small talk that quickly establishes a relationship.

In the interview process, small talk is one way to break the ice and establish some rapport. The interviewer hopes to unlock your deepest secrets in the search for the 'perfect' recruit, and you hope to make an initially favourable impression. This final point is important – there's plenty of research that shows that interviewers form a strong, initial impression of a candidate in the first few minutes of the interview.

When it comes to small talk we are our own worst critics. One common reason some of us dislike small talk (and this is usually more true of men than women) is that we feel there's no point to the conversation – 'I just can't chat about nothing'. You may really be saying that you just do not want to make the effort – or take the risk of doing it less than adequately. But small talk is a skill you can acquire: the more you do it, the better you get at it.

Effective small talk in the interview process, while triggering your active listening mode, achieves several important objectives:

1. It allows the organization to appear to be '**people-oriented**' through personal attention to the candidate.
2. It sets a **tone of goodwill and positive feelings** that enhances the interview and encourages the applicant to relax and be more open.

3. It allows the candidate to create a favourable opening impression as someone who 'fits in'.

Interviewers have a responsibility to the organization to screen in all the applicants that they feel are serious candidates who meet the qualifications for the position – possessing the knowledge, skills, abilities to do the job, along with the motivation – and who are interpersonal 'fits'. Yet they will always *feel* strongly inclined towards candidates who appear relaxed, self-assured, and who give off the message 'I sound as if I will fit in here very comfortably'.

Interviewing and 'Dating'

Think of the recruitment process as a courtship and the interview as a date. Both the interviewer and the job applicant are determining whether or not the relationship should go further. Sharing some facts about you on a first date may scare the other person away immediately. In casual discussions – such as talking to the person next to you on a plane – what works well is to **gradually share** information on a mutual basis. If one party discloses and the other does not, the informal rules of conversation tell you there is an imbalance - and an ineffective exchange results.

An interview uses an adapted version of social rules, but rapport tends to build when there is at least the *appearance* of mutual disclosure. You are invited to gradually reveal aspects of yourself which may be of interest or value to a decision-maker. As in dating, if too much is disclosed too quickly, the person receiving the information is overwhelmed and becomes concerned with what he or she has just learned. It's important to remember that the interviewer is interested in absorbing only as much information as is required for each step in the process.

- *Don't get too detailed*: Don't give a 10-minute explanation of your journey when asked 'How was the trip here?'.
- *Don't respond aggressively*: 'What's that got to do with the job?'
- *Don't get too personal*: 'I've just gone through another messy divorce.'

Understand and appreciate this fact so that you disclose neither too much nor too little information at any given point in the interview. Don't, for example, go into elaborate and technical detail about the intricacies of a position, boring the interviewer to the extent that the interviewer dismisses you as over-talkative.

Opening the Interview

Look for small talk opportunities. You may be the initiator or you may not. Once inside the organization, you are likely to come in contact initially with reception or security staff. Chat with them – it's a good, informal opportunity to warm yourself up for the real thing and you may discover some useful background about the company. During the day you may get the chance to meet people assigned to the department where you may be working. Use the opportunity to show interests, ask useful questions, and establish relationships – these people may well be asked the question 'Do you feel you could work with X?'.

These exchanges also warm up your listening skills. 'Ice-breakers' should trigger your listening skills and get you set for the real business of the interview. This is particularly important early in the day because you have probably spent the time leading up to the interview getting ready for this meeting in isolation. The more you make conscientious attempts to hear and listen to what is going on around you, the more prepared you are when the interview commences to listen to what is being said.

You can initiate small talk too. You are not confined to responding to questions. This may be an opportunity to comment on something you have seen in the waiting area – whether the subject is organization-related or not. If the person you are meeting with (or the department) is mentioned, certainly give it a try without being obsequious. Another technique is to comment on something the organization is doing for the community: '*I see your company has strong links with the High School – I've been a Governor there for two years now.*' This is the opportunity for the interviewer to ask questions and to search for similarities in approach and challenges.

Seek Personal 'Hooks'

Experienced salespeople will tell you that they get great results by establishing a warm relationship at this early contact point. This means looking for personal 'hooks' – in other words, things that are not entirely work-related that you have in common. If an interviewer is wearing a lapel badge for an organization or charity you support, it's appropriate to make a comment. Naturally, if your interviewer's office is festooned with sports memorabilia or pictures of vintage sports cars, it would be socially odd not to make some kind of comment. If you can establish something you have in common, that works well. A word of warning: be careful about commenting on family photographs. You have no idea if the person interviewing you has been bereaved, divorced, or is highly sensitive to personal comments.

Look for Openers

You can use all kinds of small talk to provide openings for conversations that quickly establish rapport, e.g. '*What a great tan. Have you been on holiday?'* Small talk can be a great assistance to your job search and can be helpful regardless of the setting. Whether you are in the beginning of an interview or en route to an appointment, you never know where the opportunity may arise of uncovering a job prospect that may develop from casual conversation started with a person that just happens to be standing next to you. You often begin by expressing an interest or asking about a line of work, and suddenly you're discovering the most useful information of all – about **real people in real jobs**. The person next to you, with whom you have just started the most casual of conversations, may even be aware of an open position. Not only might you pursue it, but you should use his or her name.

Avoid Controversial Topics at All Costs

It's generally unwise to initiate talk on controversial topics from today's newspaper, particularly relating to politics, religion or ethics. You have no idea where your interviewer stands on such topics. One thing is clear: if you immediately communicate something that indicates you hold strong views that are completely opposite to those of the interviewer, it does very little for your employment prospects.

Questions, Questions...

Throughout this chapter and the rest of the book, you'll find sequences of typical interview questions with supporting commentary and, where appropriate, an example answer. They begin here.

Q2   What do you think of this weather?

Don't get into complex discussion of meteorology and long-term forecasts. Even in these controversial times, people can still agree that there is nothing you can do about the weather. It's normal to complain about it, but not for too long. People who complain endlessly about the weather usually complain about many other things when they get the chance.

Q3   Did you have a hard time finding the office? Did your train come in on time? How was your hotel?

Again a typical low order question. Don't give boring details. You may find this a useful opportunity to disclose something useful. For example, in response to '**Did you have trouble finding us?**' your response may be '*No – my gym is just across the street.*' The interviewer then has an opportunity to ask a follow-up question such as '**How often do you get there?**'. Inserting this kind of data personally, instead of on your CV, allows you to be spontaneous and take advantage of any 'clues' in the office of the interviewer (a photo of the interviewer completing the London marathon, for example).

Consider very carefully your responses to any questions about your arrival if they included travel arrangements made on your behalf by the employer. You want to avoid commenting negatively on poor travel planning or choice of hotel. In the worst situation of totally messed-up reservations, it's still diplomatic to say '*The arrangements were perfect – I got here without a hitch*'. With that comment you accomplish two things: You pretty much close the discussion on the topic extremely quickly since you are hoping to move on to more important issues (namely yourself and their job opening) and the tone you set is totally positive. It is a small issue, and you pay a compliment to those responsible. You cannot lose with that response. If the interviewer has had terrible experiences with the same train route or hotel, you will register that you are flexible enough to cope with difficulties.

However, *if you were late for the interview* (due to their misdirections or your own errors), keep the problems to yourself. Don't hope your lateness hasn't been noticed just because it's not your fault. Apologize quickly (this may have been their agenda in raising the question) and accept the responsibility yourself, putting the blame if appropriate on outside factors such as the traffic or weather.

'First of all, I'm terribly sorry for being late. I should have antici-pated how difficult the rush hour can be.'

Q4　What do you think of this city/town?

Presumably your job search has not precluded your reading newspapers or watching news programmes. If you are travel-ling to another city, try to read a local paper in advance to determine what is in the news. You won't be expected to have an in-depth knowledge of local issues, but you should know something about major issues such as the rise or fall of major employers, or social issues such as radical new measures to control traffic. A local newspaper provides insights into the location as a place for you to live and may even give you some clues about the local community and social problems.

*Q5　I saw on your CV that you enjoy _____. How did you get interested in this?

Once you have provided any information on your CV, it is fair game for a line of enquiry. Interests are far more likely to come up in the interview process if your work experience is limited. Indeed, if this is the case, you may want to ensure that you have some useful information in the 'Interests' part of your CV.

　Consider your answer in advance, and make it brief. It's a good idea to show active choice and planning rather than an idea that suggests you passively or haphazardly jump into things ('Oh, I went along with a friend and it seemed quite interesting'). At the same time phrase the answer to imply that you are always open to the new and different but that golf or coin collecting never gets into the way of job performance.

Don't forget that this kind of question can helpfully open up opportunities for you to demonstrate links between voluntary activities and the workplace:

'I spend a lot of my time working as a Scout Leader. It's great fun, and very demanding. One of the things people often don't realize about Scouting is that you get access to some excellent management training...'

Including this type of information may be more trouble than it's worth. Never claim interests that you don't really hold, or only hold lightly. Why take the risk of exposing yourself as a charlatan on a job-irrelevant issue like hobbies or special interests when there is no reason to, if you run into an argumentative 'expert'. If you are perceived to be dishonest on this point, everything you've put in your work history will seem untrue. Include on your CV only hobbies or interests:

■ You can talk about enthusiastically, answering follow-up questions from someone with an avid interest in the same topic
■ Which have some direct relevance to the organization (e.g. surfing if you're after a job with a watersports company), or which communicate employment-related skills such as leadership or teamwork
■ Which communicate your skills (e.g. fund-raising, organizing, public speaking)
■ Which strongly demonstrate personal qualities such as active choice, painstaking research, dedication, commitment.

Q6   I see that you also went to _____ [university/college]. How is Professor ___ these days? I see you went to ____. I went there myself. Do they still ____?

Share the answer if you know it. If you do not, admit it without apology but with a brief explanation of why you do not know. You may have studied a different course and may have had no contact with this professor or lecturer. Do not go on the defensive, pretend you know when you don't, and have to worry about the next question. If you keep up with the alumni association or have a family member attending the same university, briefly share this with the interviewer. Don't complain about your education; your interviewer may be someone who would have jumped at the chance to study at your university or follow the course you did.

Q7   How do you like living in ____?

Be positive. Even if it is the worst place in the world, try in advance to identify something about it that can be mentioned in an attractive light. You may wish to give a balanced opinion, for example when talking about a big city: '*It's a terrific place because of the huge range of people you meet, but it's a nightmare if you want to park your car.*' By making the statement and being brief, you are showing your interest in addressing the question directly and giving it importance because the interviewer has determined it is important enough to ask.

Be cautious if the job you are looking at may require a relocation. If you enthuse about living in the town which is presently home, you're communicating an unspoken '*and I don't want to leave it*'.

While answering, watch interviewers for non-verbal clues to determine whether they agree or disagree. If they have heard enough, the line of questioning ends there. If they want to know more and your reply has stirred more interest, they will continue with a follow-up question.

Q8 I see that you are reading ___ [book/magazine/paper]. What do you think of it?

Just as we mentioned when discussing the inclusion of interests and hobbies on the CV, you control what you share with the interviewer through oral and written communication. Don't forget disclosure goes beyond that. Your whole appearance sends a message. That includes anything that you carry with you (bag, briefcase, and anything in them that you take out and show to anyone during the process).

If there are a range of newspapers in the waiting room, pick up the one that you might normally read (unless it is totally inappropriate for the job you are after). If you want to show you read *The Economist* or the *Financial Times*, you might bring a copy along and read it while waiting – but only do so if this is a publication you read normally. You may be asked about a regular feature or contributor, and your lack of familiarity with this topic sends out the wrong message.

The same is true for any other publication or book. Once you choose to use it, you are fair game to be tested on your knowledge of it. Again, if you're asked to comment on a book you are reading, give a very short response – not a book review.

Q9 I see that you drive a _____. How do you get on with it?

This question indicates two things about interviewers. First, they want to show that they noticed the vehicle you are driving. Second, they want you to know that they recognized it and thought it important enough to ask you a question about it. Whether or not the only purpose for the question is to ask a small talk question to set you at ease, treat it as such and be brief and to the point. If it is the worst car you have ever owned, do not let on. Be positive. If the car looks a wreck or has a terrible reputation (deserved or not), consider borrowing someone else's vehicle for the meeting or parking away from the office. Some people, sadly, measure others by the vehicle they drive (or the place they live); the vehicle chosen becomes one more opportunity to judge the choice made by the applicant.

The question may actually be geared to company cars – in which case you may be told something about the package on offer. Express a mild interest rather than interrogating the listener on the precise specification of car on offer. The question may also be a covert opportunity for the interviewer to tell you about his or her brand new car – in which case you now have an excellent personal 'hook'.

Q10   What do you think of our new office/factory/building?

Here again, say something positive. You may be talking to the person who designed the whole thing, or the main critic of the new scheme. Don't gush or pretend you're an expert in architecture or design, but say one or two relatively positive things about the way the building 'feels'. If you see a floor layout, production line, display or any other kind of facility that is clearly innovative and well-designed, indicate your admiration.

Q11   What do you prefer to be called?

This is a considerate question that indicates the interviewer wishes to make you comfortable by calling you the way you wished to be called. 'Christopher' might be 'Chris' or 'Kit', and might equally hate any form of abbreviation at all. Interviewers show their concern by acknowledging that something as simple as a name is not to be taken for granted. If you really prefer one version over others and it is important to you, even if the question is not asked, mention it but don't be fussy or long-winded about it: '*Christopher is fine*' is far preferable to '*I really hate it when people call me Chris*'. Interviewers who cannot say your name as requested, even after you mention it, may be poor listeners, and you may have an early clue that you need to work hard to get your message across.

One more comment: If your name is so important to you, don't forget to share that information as soon as you can, including taking the opportunity before the meeting. There's no need to put your full name on your CV, particularly if your first name isn't the name you're known by. If you are very commonly known by a nickname, you may indicate this on a covering letter or right at the beginning. A big smile, an offered handshake and '*My friends call me Bill*' makes life easier for the interviewer and lowers barriers. If any of your names are difficult to pronounce, give the interviewer some help. If your nickname is twee or strange ('CJ', or even 'Animal'), strongly consider keeping this to yourself until you're in place.

When this question is asked the interviewer is usually seeking permission to use your first name. If the relationship warms up reasonably well you might feel free to do the same in return – it depends on the formality of the occasion and how senior the interviewer is.

Q12   What do you think about _____ [any controversial 'in the news' topic]?

This is a question that may crop up during the small talk portion of the interview. It is a chance for the interviewer to see if you are keeping up with current events, or it may just be friendly banter on a topic that you would have to be dead to have no knowledge about. *The commencement of this seemingly innocuous line of enquiry may provide an opportunity for inter-viewers to probe into your beliefs and political opinions to deter-mine if those views are acceptable.* Show that you are informed but try to avoid taking sides, before and after interviewers reveal their views of the issue – if they choose to do so. By staying above giving an opinion, you demonstrate balance and objectivity. Don't give too much away at first about your opinion, and under no circumstances should you communi-cate the idea that your mind is closed to issues, since this communicates inflexibility and a lack of willingness to learn.

The one exception here is if you're approaching an organiza-tion which has clear and strong views on an issue, perhaps because it is a charity or lobbying organization. In these circumstances you'll need to show which side of the fence you're on, but here again you also need to demonstrate the ability to see things from other perspectives – even committed reforming organizations need good communicators, not bigots.

Q13   Would you like something to drink?

Some cultures use an offer of a drink as an opportunity to demonstrate hospitality. In the UK and Europe it's rare to be offered alcohol in an interview, unless your conversation is over lunch or dinner. In this case, **always take your lead from the interviewer**. If the interviewer orders Perrier and you ask for a double brandy, you're clearly out of tune.

In most interviews a 'drink' means tea, coffee or water. Do not become hung up on the idea that the offer has hidden meanings. It doesn't, but it does present problems: you now have to juggle a cup and saucer as well as your pen and papers. Best to accept a drink if waiting in reception and decline the offer of a drink in the interview itself. This is not a social call. If you really are too parched to speak, ask for a glass of water, take a good sip, and then put it down some-where you won't knock it over.

Q14   Is there anything else you need?

Don't ask for an ashtray. In fact, don't smoke unless you are specifically invited to do so and all the interviewers present are also lighting up. Under no circumstances should you ask to smoke. You may be in a no-smoking area, or you may be talking to people who hate the smell of cigarettes (so air your clothes well before going to an interview). You may be well advised to suppress the impulse to have a cigarette in the car park just before the interview, simply because your clothes will smell of smoke.

Be aware that many organizations now find it difficult to accommodate smokers – both in terms of facilities and team preferences. Don't give the interviewer a reason to exclude you. If you need the nicotine, smoke outside before you go into the building.

Big Points about Small Talk

- Small talk allows the interjection of the **human element** into the interview process, which can otherwise be very formal or mechanistic.
- Your ability to handle and generate small talk may well be taken as an indication of your ability to mix well in a team, with other members of staff, and with customers. Don't try going for a customer-facing role, for example, without demonstrating the ability to show an interest in others and win them over quickly.
- The willingness of the interviewer to engage in any chit-chat before the line of direct questions opens can be a strong indication of the **way the company feels about people**. It will certainly be a swift indication of the personality and style of the person interviewing you – who may eventually be your line manager.
- If you are the slightest ill at ease talking about 'nothing', **practise**. Start light conversations on bank lines, while shopping, and in waiting rooms. You never know what you will discover.

- **Stay clear of controversial topics** regardless of how the topic is introduced.
- Remember the power of **first impressions** – what you say at the beginning of the interview will often be taken as a strong indication of your overall qualities. Small talk helps you to provide up-front, positive evidence about your personality and interpersonal skills.

6 Getting *Your* Message Across

SELLING YOURSELF

Once you have secured a job interview, the next stage is to manage your behaviours and the perceptions of the interviewer, and to secure a job offer. This means learning about listening, non-verbal communication, and above all being aware of what you are communicating during the interview.

What Do I Have to Communicate?

The art of communication in interviews is *sharing the information you want to remain in the interviewer's mind*. It is up to you to decide how much information you wish to share, the extent you choose to share it, and how you want to share it. You may disclose something consciously (by deciding in advance what you want to say) or non-verbally (especially when your body language contradicts the words you are using). Any time a question is asked – whatever the setting – in providing the answer, you determine consciously or unconsciously how much information you choose to share with the person raising the question. Share too much too quickly, and others may back away because you are sharing more than they want to hear. Share too little or too slowly, and others may feel that you are being unfriendly. They may consider withdrawing from the encounter because their attempts at conversation are not being answered sufficiently.

Interviews and 'Chats'

If any employer says to you 'it won't be an interview – just a chat', be cautious. There's no such thing as a 'chat' in recruitment. No matter how informal, it's an interview. An interview is a kind of conversation, but an odd kind of conversation; it's a conversation which has a particular structure, a very clear purpose, and one where one person is very much in control. It can be confusing because an interview mimics informal conversation (smiling, showing an interest in the other person, listening, encouraging someone to speak and feel comfortable), but unlike a conversation with your friends over coffee, this is an interaction that can affect the next 10 years of your life.

Why an Interviewer Wants to Get You to Open Up

The objective of any conversation is to exchange information at a level that is appropriate and acceptable to both parties. Just as in social settings, in an interview there is an unstated agreement between the two participants that, if sufficient and applicable information is supplied by the applicant, the interviewer reciprocates by letting the recruitment and selection process continue and ultimately by making the job offer. An interviewer wants you to open up and *disclose* information about you that isn't apparent from your CV – your personality, your motivation, the way you carry out your skills.

As a result, interviewers are trained to encourage you to 'open up' during the interview process. They want you to feel comfortable enough to disclose things that you won't say if you remain defensive. This has both positive and negative aspects. On the one hand, if you get on with the person interviewing and really establish a rapport, you significantly increase your chances of a job offer. On the negative side, disclosure can also mean that you are persuaded to present negative information which gives the recruiter a reason *not* to appoint you.

Interviewers have various techniques to open you up like a book. They begin by asking you 'low order' questions – in other words, straightforward questions that you don't really need to think about very much. Right at the beginning of the interview an interviewer is making social noises, things like 'isn't the weather dreadful today?' or even the slightly absurd 'did you get here all right?'.

Subsequently you'll find that an interviewer's main tool for getting you to talk freely is the *open question*. Essentially this is a question that you can't answer with 'yes', 'no', or a simple fact. Closed questions like 'did you enjoy that?' don't open candidates up, but sometimes you'll be asked a good closed question that establishes facts: 'when did you qualify?' Good open questions often begin 'Tell me about...'. They are encouraging you to talk – but not for ever! Throughout this book we'll look at the need for controlled, brief responses.

Experience vs Potential: Which One Matters?

While working out your principal message, you may wonder which is more important – experience or potential? A senior financial recruiter remarked that one of the frustrating aspects of the job search process is that, depending on the background and role of the interviewer, either one might matter more than the other. Is the employer looking for someone who has done the job well before, or someone who will grow into the job?

The picture depends a great deal on the perceptions of the interviewer and his or her organizational position. Frequently, human resource staff insist on short-listing only those candidates that meet the line manager's job requirements exactly. Line managers, on the other hand, are usually more flexible in considering candidates. 'Fit' and attractiveness (i.e. total presentation) may be weighed more heavily than skill level and actual experience.

Ultimately, once you've won the interview, the main thing that matters is that you demonstrate both the right experience and potential. What's even more important is that you **don't talk yourself out of the job.**

Which Matters More – Experience or Potential?

Experience	Potential
Interviewed by HR	Interviewed by line managers or business owner
Looking to match existing criteria	Looking to solve existing problems in a range of ways
Concerned about internal credibility	Able to offer something different
Already capable of doing the job	Will grow into the job, and may be more motivated as a result

Tricks of the Trade – Techniques Interviewers Will Use on You

Trained interviewers will normally begin with **low order questions** (see **Chapter 5**) – ice-breakers to get the conversation flowing (e.g. 'How was your trip in this morning?'). As the interview progresses, they will increase the pace and switch to **high order questions**. These questions are designed to make you think, to probe your experience, and to get behind your first, glib answer. High order questions often require a couple of seconds' thinking time – so don't be afraid of pausing and reflecting.

Well trained interviewers will listen carefully to your responses and *then dig underneath* what you say with a particular kind of high order question – the **probing question**. This throws badly-prepared candidates who only have a superficial grasp of their own evidence. A probe checks what you really did, and the problems you had to overcome. A question may also probe parts of your experience you are not too happy about discussing. Probing questions can open the door to an entire chain of related questions. Prepare for them by looking at all the information on your CV and all the extra pieces of evidence you intend to put forward (see **Presentation Statements** below), and imagine that an interviewer drills down several levels by asking those questions you just don't want to hear.

The interviewer's main tools during the interview process are **open** and **closed** questions, as in the table below.

Open Questions	Closed Questions
■ Leave respondents open to answer however they wish (e.g. 'Tell me about your present job')	■ May require a yes/no answer (e.g. 'Do you enjoy this kind of work'?)
■ Encourage candidates to disclose and communicate freely (e.g. 'What did you enjoy most about that job?')	■ May be used to contain an over-talkative candidate (e.g. 'Just let me check: what profit margin did you actually achieve?')
■ May be probing (e.g. 'Why did you leave your last job?')	■ May be used to check facts (e.g. 'How many staff did you supervise?')
■ If done well, will draw out a candidate's relevant experience and achievements	■ May simply check a date or number (e.g. 'When did you qualify?')

Here is an example of a sequence of questions that an interviewer could use:

- Question 1: '*Do you work overtime in your present job?*' A closed question to establish the simple facts with the briefest of replies ('yes', 'no', 'sometimes', or 'depends').
  '*Yes.*'
- Question 2: '*What causes the overtime to occur?*' Open to give you the option of analysing the reasons from your experience.
- Question 3: '*On what basis are the workers chosen to work overtime?*' Another open question that allows you to elaborate.
- Question 4: '*Why might you have problems working overtime?*' The interviewer has now established some facts and now starts to probe.
  '*It wouldn't normally be a problem.*'
- Question 5: '*Under what circumstances might it be a problem?*' The probe goes deeper. There's no way out except to be very specific and turn a doubt in the interviewer's mind into a positive:

'*Naturally I'd want to help the company out, particularly if the reason was increased orders. If I can have 48 hours notice, I'd be available for overtime.*'

The Killer Pause

A technique that may throw you slightly is where the interviewer allows a silence after you have given a short response. You need to be very clear whether you need to carry on. Sometimes a pause like this will draw unwary candidates into saying rather too much. See **Presentation Statements** later in this chapter to learn how to prepare and rehearse short responses to the most difficult questions – and remember to shut up when you've finished! An interviewer will always make it clear if you haven't provided enough information. Sometimes a pause occurs simply because the interviewer is digesting what you have just said, or thinking up the next question. If you speak, you're interrupting the flow of the interview. In general, learn to say less and make what you say effective and appropriate.

Summarizing

Another technique used by experienced interviewers is summarizing. This may just happen at the end, or may happen at different stages of the interview (particularly with a well trained interviewer).

A good summary will be very helpful to you in establishing what the interviewer has actually heard and understood. You will also get some interesting clues about the information that the interviewer values. Don't be afraid to respond to a summary:

'Yes, that's all correct. What I haven't mentioned is that I also had purchasing responsibility in my first job – I had to put together the company's first preferred suppliers list.'

Dry Runs

Identify several skills, experiences or behaviours that you feel are essential to your candidacy. Then write a scenario with open, closed and probing questions designed to elicit information from you. For example, if computer literacy is a key issue, the following exchange is likely to occur:

Questions about Your IT Experience

Open: 'What software do you use on a regular basis?'

For each program you identify, provide what output you generate with it.

Closed: 'Are you responsible for designing reports or only for generating reports that are designed by others?'

Open: 'What are your biggest problems with the software you are using?'

Probing: 'What's the most difficult thing you've achieved using this piece of software?'

Closed: 'Are there other software packages that would be more effective?'

Open: 'What are they and in what way will they be more effective?'

Closed: 'Do you have a PC at home?'

Open: 'What do you use it for?'

Guide to Handling Open and Closed Questions

- **Practise** whenever you can to develop a series of related questions on any topic by mixing all question types.
- Closed questions **focus you on a topic** and open questions **dig deeper for content**.
- Try to **anticipate open questions** when the conversation begins with innocuous closed questions.
- Respond with detail, but not too much. The interviewer may be happy with your initial response if it is focused. Saying too much increases the chance of introducing negative ideas and information.
- Anticipate where an interviewer is going to **probe**. Imagine that each piece of information you put in front of the interviewer is like bait on a fish hook. Which answers are going to make the interviewer bite?

*Q15 Talk me through your work history...

You've probably already provided this information in your application form or CV, but you should be able to take an interviewer through your history, step by step, but at a reasonable pace. Be prepared to talk about positions you have held, what you leaned from them, and be specific about job titles, dates and job responsibilities. Keep it interesting, and try to talk about something that connects all the jobs you've done – possibly something about what you have learned, or what the jobs have in common.

Think about what the interviewer already has available (application form or CV), and try to speak in a way that makes the document come alive.

'I think there's a thread that links all the jobs that I've done, and it's an interest in developing people. I started my working life as a lecturer, but then moved through a series of commercial training roles. More recently I've managed a training department and commissioned a number of major new projects. Perhaps it would help if I tell you a little about the job I've done most recently...'

Be consistent about details. Particular areas are dates and job titles. Be aware of obvious 'gaps' in your work history that an interviewer will ask you about.

Presentation Statements

There are some areas of questioning that you know will come up in the interview, and you wish they wouldn't. These are areas where you are vulnerable. If you are asked these kinds of questions you are more likely to stumble, to blush, and to come up with an inadequate answer. You'll probably say too much, and say something that will plant a negative idea in the interviewer's mind. What these questions are will vary from one person to another, but here are some examples of typical questions that press most people's buttons (the question numbers in this book are printed alongside):

> There appears to be a gap of six months/years on your CV.
> What were you doing during this time? (Q23)
>
> Who's the most difficult manager you've ever had to deal
> with? (Q32)
>
> What are your strengths? What are your weaknesses? (Q38)
>
> Why do you want to leave your present job? (Q52)
>
> How long have you been looking for a job? (Q56)
>
> Where do you hope to be in five years' time? (Q67)
>
> What have you learned in the last 12 months? (Q79)
>
> What was the result of your last appraisal? (Q108)
>
> Have you ever been fired? Describe the circumstances. (Q168)
>
> Why aren't you earning more at your age? (Q178)
>
> Learn **Presentation Statements** to cope with any questions
> like this. Write them down – it makes a difference. A presenta-
> tion statement is a short, well-practised answer that gets you
> past this point in the interview. All you need to do is to be brief
> and positive, and the interviewer will usually move on and be
> reasonably satisfied.

Q16 Why were you made redundant from your last job?

This is an ideal example of a question that requires a reasonably well-rehearsed Presentation Statement. An interviewer
does not want to hear about how hurt you feel, how badly
you were treated, or exactly where you are up to in your
dispute over your redundancy payment. All the interviewer
needs to hear is that there wasn't and isn't a problem:

*'It was a major restructuring and a number of us were laid off at
the same time. These things happen. Actually, it's been a good
opportunity to move into something different...'*

Q17 How did you get your last job?

Was your last job move planned, or did something just come
along? Planning a career move demonstrates to the interviewer

your sense of direction and purpose, and it indicates that you are a person who plans and takes action. If you stumbled upon your last job, the answer is just not as strong regardless of the circumstances. You need to prepare a polished answer that presents the situation in the best light possible, ideally linking it to the present position by demonstrating that you have a strong picture of how you want your career to come together.

If the question is 'How did you come across us?', your response should be equally cautious. If the company should be well known to you because of your immersion in a particular field of work, you'll get no brownie points by saying '*through your job ad*'. If you hadn't come across the company before, think of reasons why you should have done. You should have no difficulty backing up these comments because of the background research you have done into the organization.

'*Clearly you've been a key player in this sector for a number of years, and I see your market share has grown considerably.*'

Q18   How did you hear about this position?

This answer demonstrates the quality of your sources of information. If your neighbour happens to be the managing director of the organization (or any other employee, for that matter), do not hesitate to mention that he or she told you about the opening. As a rule, internal introductions work effectively because they demonstrate that you are known to the company. On the other hand, do not portray the referral as something it isn't. If you have no connection directly to the staff member, be honest about it. Once the person is mentioned, the interviewer is very likely to pursue the comment to determine the nature of the relationship. It is better to hear it from you now than from the employee later.

Q19   Have you received any other job offers? What other organizations or positions are you considering?

Employers like job applicants who are actively sought by others. Once you admit that you have other offers pending, you need to be careful not to disclose the wrong information. Some employers have disdain and outright scorn for competitors and others in the marketplace. You certainly don't want to give the impression that you're looking for the highest bidder. Better to vaguely indicate that you're having some interesting conversations with other companies, but nothing is 'official' yet. That way you shouldn't be asked to name specific organizations. The danger is that you mention the wrong kind of organization (too small, too traditional...) which suddenly puts you in the wrong kind of light as far as the interviewer is concerned.

'I've got to final interview stage for a number of positions, but what I believe this organization has to offer which others don't is a tremendous learning opportunity.'

Q20   What do you enjoy doing outside work?

This is not being asked idly as part of small talk in the opening of the interview, and this kind of question is not limited to those who are relatively new to the job market. The question is there to seek a broader picture of your personality. There are two points not to be missed: First, **your response could 'define' you** to the interviewer. What you choose to do may say a lot about who you are. Are you active (*'avid runner'*) or passive (*'spectator'*), a loner (*'write poetry'*) or a joiner (*'Round Table'*)? Second, the person interviewing you may have a **particular interest in what you say**. Be prepared to discuss the subject in more detail if called on to do so. If you do not want to open this door, omit the information from your CV and application forms. And whatever you put under 'interests' in your CV, make sure that it is either relevant to the job or something you can talk about enthusiastically for five minutes if pushed.

If you are considering a job in a sports clothing retailers, having an interest in canoeing or climbing would be a useful related interest. Do not mention too many because you may be perceived as having too many demands on your time already. For example, mention golf if your research confirms that golf is a major corporate pastime, if business is generated with relationships developed during 18 holes of golf, and, above all, *if you already play reasonably well.* Do not under any circumstances pretend to be something you are not ; a knowledgeable interviewer could discover your fiction in seconds. Remember that an interviewer will often assume that *a candidate who lies or exaggerates around one area of experience will do so around all areas of experience.*

Q21   What are you doing now to attain a goal you have set for yourself?

Start the answer with a definition of the goal. It may be job-related ('... *to move to the next position within one year*') or not ('... *to get the degree I have postponed for so long*'). Once the goal has been defined, be ready to demonstrate how you have started to go about it. If you can include a timeframe, do so. It demonstrates all the more forcefully that your planning is specific rather than just a dream.

Q22   What is your current salary?

Tread carefully. There are three ways to consider this question:

1. *Did you fill out an application?* If so, they already have the information, so be consistent.
2. Do you know the salary range for the open position (from

the job ad, a recruiter, or insider information)? Answer with a range, if possible ('Mid-thirties before commissions'). **Negotiate salary when the job is offered, not before.**

3. *You have no idea what the open position pays.* If you come in too low, you may be taken up at a 'cheap' price; too high, and you have priced yourself out of the job. Couch your response by giving an accurate amount, and if you feel it is too low, add, '*That is base salary exclusive of perks and benefits that are quite generous and should be considered a part of a total compensation package.*'

If the question is phrased '*What do you feel this position should pay?*' it is easier to deal with, but it is still stressful because salary is always a delicate topic. In this instance, you should try to defer it if you do not have a reasonable understanding of the position's responsibilities and scope. You may also ask for assistance from the interviewer. Ask if there are similar positions in the organization, and probe the salary range. Once the interviewer shares some information (unless the position is truly unique, which is very rare), you may project for this position not so much a salary, but a salary range.

In principle, this is a simple fact-checking question that is difficult to duck. If pressed, give an honest answer but follow it up with a clear statement of intent: '*I'm paid £XX but I'm currently being interviewed for positions at a rather higher level.*'

Q23 There appears to be a gap of six months/two years on your CV. What were you doing during this time?

You should be prepared to respond to this question if you take the time before interview to consider your activities both on and off the job. **Make your answer crisp, brief, focused on the point, and not defensive.** That kind of answer portrays you as a person who does what you have to do.

'Constant care of a family member required someone's attention and the choice was between my spouse and myself. Because she had just started a new career, I decided to volunteer for the assignment.'

Q24 Do you have any objections to psychological testing?

You will generally not be given much choice in this matter, but if you are asked and you have no objections, say so directly. The employer may be using one or more tests as part of their selection process. Try to find out in advance what kind of tests you will be taking, and ideally take the opportunity to try out typical questions. If you object to this kind of testing you will generally exclude yourself from the selection process. Best to respond openly and co-operatively, but ask for full details of the kind of test you will be given, what the tests are designed to find out, and what kind of feedback you will be given. Always ask for one-to-one verbal feedback on any tests you take – you may find the results very helpful.

Q25 How does this job compare with others you are applying for?

If you mention others, then you have disclosed, perhaps without realizing it, that you may not be as interested in this position as you led the interviewer to believe. On the other hand, if you answer that you are considering only this position, then the interviewer realizes that you have little or no choice. The unasked questions here are *how marketable are you* and *how committed are you to this job?*

As far as this interviewer is concerned, this job is your number one choice. You may start by hedging, *'This is a unique position because it...'*, but continue by saying why this job and this company appeal to you and are a great match for your skills and qualities. By keeping your answer to the position being discussed, you are neither admitting nor denying the existence of other opportunities under consideration.

Q26   How did you come across this job?

This is where you rely on some good record-keeping. You should at least have a copy of the job advertisement, and you should have asked for a job description (even if one wasn't sent to you as a matter of course). It's not vital that you remember exactly where you saw the job ad, but it reflects very badly on you if you can recall nothing about how you came across the position. If you can't recall where or when, at least be clear about the job content:

'I saw the job advertisement, and I was particularly interested in the fact that you're looking for a mix of IT knowledge and general management experience.'

Q27   What is your overall impression of your last job/employer?

These are easy questions to deal with. Be upbeat and professional, and steer a careful line between analysis and enthusiasm.

'It was a great opportunity for personal growth. After three years of doing the same thing and a downturn in the industry, I saw the writing on the wall and that is why I am looking now.'

'I was fortunate to have the opportunity to work with such a great group of dedicated professionals. Unfortunately, technology passed them by and the management of the organization has yet to respond to the challenge of a changed market.'

A Word About Jargon

If your interviewer lacks experience in your specialism, don't swamp him or her with jargon. The use of this technical, 'insider' language can be a way of speaking the right 'code', but it can also be off-putting and can alienate interviewers rather than impress them. If you want to use jargon, be sure you are current and up-to-date, and be prepared for probing questions designed to check that you really understand what you are talking about. You may of course need to respond to some jargon being used by an interviewer to check if you really know your stuff. Generally it's better to speak in plain English – it certainly communicates your ability to explain your job to non-specialists.

Q28 Can we contact your present/former employer for a reference?

If you are presently employed, you probably don't want your employers knowing about your job search until you have given notice. State, '*I will be very pleased to provide excellent references from my current employer if a position is offered. If you wish to contact any of my former employers please let me know before you do so.*' It is a mark of professional courtesy for you to notify any of the referees that you have provided, of the names and organizations that will be contacting them.

Regardless of the circumstances, **never lie** about events, employment records or your personal history. It is a small world and the facts come to light eventually (or you will get an ulcer worrying about their discovery). In any event, if you include something false on a signed application form it can be grounds for dismissal.

Q29 What kind of position are you looking for – permanent, temporary or interim?

In the not too distant past, jobs were simple. There were those looking for permanent jobs and then a very small group who really preferred a temporary or contract job because of their unique personal or professional needs. Actors wanted temporary work so that they would be able to audition for parts whenever called upon to do so. Others who sought temping included those between circumstances: someone waiting for a spouse to be settled in a new location, a student waiting to start university.

All that has changed. More people now seek temporary employment in order to allow them to pursue other interests that may be income-producing or not. Another group of people are working in temporary jobs involuntarily – that is, because they are unable to secure regular full-time employment.

If you are interested only in temporary work and you say so, interviewers may dismiss your application because they need employees who are willing to stay. On the other hand, if the interviewer wants to hire employees on a contingency basis, and you say you want a permanent job, then the interviewer may lose interest in you.

If a permanent job is what you truly want, you do not lose by stating your preference directly. The best technique is to get the employer to talk about the **problem** that the job is trying to solve: *'Ideally I'd like a permanent position, but I'm really interested in working here, so I'm happy to look at alternatives. Why don't we start by looking at what you need? What problems are you dealing with?'* Talking about 'alternatives' makes you flexible without committing yourself to a particular pattern, and it's always important to show that you're interested in the organization. However, consider your answer carefully beforehand because it offers your potential employer the opportunity to delay a 'permanent' offer, because you are already conceding to a 'look and see' approach.

Look at the employer's biggest headaches and greatest opportunities, and try to agree how the role can make a difference. If you do this well enough, you may persuade the organization to make an interim position permanent. Employers are often far more flexible about this than you think – but remember that the best time to negotiate terms is after the job offer.

Top 10 Rules for Every Interview

1. Be on time.
2. **Dress the part**. Look like you already work there.
3. Smile occasionally (not that look from the film *The Shining*). Aim for an awake, alert, pleasant, open appearance.
4. **Keep it conversational**. *Do not sound rehearsed, even if it is.*
5. **Keep your purpose in mind**. What are your main points? What can you do for this organization?
6. **Accentuate the positive**. Put negative aspects in the best light.
7. **Give details.** Quantify. (Size of your staff? Expense reductions? Sales increase?)
8. **Do not give monologues**. Ideal answers are from 30 seconds to two minutes. Interviews should be 50–50 conversations. Don't feel you need to tell them your life story. As in advertising and marketing, you don't have to give every detail of a product to induce a sale – just enough strong points to satisfy the buyers' demands.
9. **Ask for the job**. State your desire to work for the organization and be specific as to why you are a perfect match for the position.
10. **Follow-up**. Send a thank-you letter for the time and consideration or make a telephone call after every interview.

7

Personality Questions

WHO ARE YOU?

The traditional job interview has always been about personality. The biographical interview looked at your past, but also tried to assess personality 'fit'. At worst, interviewers are highly subjective about selecting people they like or (worse still) people like them. Many modern methods of interviewing tend to stick far more closely to questions relating to work, but even in the most carefully structured competency-based interview (see **Chapter 11**) the selection decision still has some connection, conscious or unconscious, with the idea *'does this individual have the right kind of personal qualities?'*. Good interviewers are interested in learning all they can about every person they interview. They have a responsibility to their employers to obtain as much information about you as you are willing to provide. They want a full understanding of what you are about – on and off the job.

Personality questions are intended to allow the interviewer to try to understand:

- How you will fit into a team or organization.
- How you might get along with particular clients or colleagues.
- How you will operate under pressure.
- What your feelings are about this organization and this position.

An important dimension of personality is **motivation**, which is discussed separately in **Chapter 8**.

Understanding EQ

An important ingredient for life success is an idea popularized by Daniel Goleman: **Emotional Intelligence**. Most of us at some stage will have had a test of our IQ. Goleman suggests that we also have a measurable 'EQ' as well. He says that there are five elements to an increased awareness of emotional intelligence:

1. **Knowing your emotions** – being able to monitor and describe a feeling as it happens.
2. **Managing emotions** – handling feelings as they arise, coping with our emotional reactions to setbacks and upsets.
3. **Motivating yourself** – marshalling emotions in the service of a personal goal.
4. **Recognizing emotions in others** – the fundamental people skill of empathy; being attuned to others' needs and the way they express them.
5. **Handling relationships** – managing and responding to emotions in others and displaying various forms of social competence; social skills, communication and leadership.

There is some argument about whether people can develop emotional intelligence. What is clear, however, is that you need to communicate how and where you are capable of using it in the workplace.

Questions on this topic may come thick and fast. How do you motivate others? Can you empathize with customers, clients, supervisors, fellow workers? Can you see another's point of view? When things get tough, boring, hectic, or chaotic at work, how do you react – and how do you help others to manage their feelings? Can you defuse emotionally charged situations? Do you know what makes you happy?

Employers, even before the term 'emotional intelligence' was coined, knew that merely having the intelligence or the skill to perform a job was not sufficient. Some experts even go so far as to attach negative emotional attributes such as 'cold,' 'calculating', 'condescending', 'inhibited', or 'fastidious' to individuals with high IQs. On the other hand, individuals with high emotional abilities are typically seen as 'cheerful', 'sympathetic', 'responsive', or 'committed' because they communicate the sense that they are happy with themselves and the people around them.

It seems clear that **emotional intelligence translates into better interpersonal skills**. You are more aware of the way your behaviours and ideas will impact on others. Staff want to work with and for people who understand them and who are able to support them.

Even if interviewers are not on the cutting edge of this theory, they know the organization needs individuals who work well together. The employment puzzle needs a good 'fit' and personal questions are needed to find out what type of fit you would make.

To relate your emotional intelligence to the position and organization that you are interviewing for, refer to the **Personal Worksheet (Chapter 2)** and now complete the **On-the-Job EQ** worksheet overleaf, filling in the specific attributes that you feel are required by the job. For example, a project manager who has to use people-influencing skills might need to be 'objective', 'analytical' and 'task-focused', but will also need to be 'flexible' and 'responsive'. Then record specific examples from your experience when you have needed to demonstrate these qualities, e.g. for 'flexible':

'One of my team took a problem away and delivered a solution using resources in another department. I indicated that I was unhappy that she had drawn other people into the project without asking, but I also stated that I was pleased that she had come up with an innovative, flexible solution.'

On-the-Job EQ

Organization:

Position:

Personal attributes needed for this position:	Specific example of when/where I exhibited this attribute:

✱ Q30   Tell me about yourself.

This is probably one of the toughest questions you will ever be asked during an interview. The difficulty is that you have no frame of reference. Are you going to talk about your history, your work experience, your goals, or your personality? The question is usually thrown in at the beginning of an interview (and may even be used to throw you off balance just a little). In some circumstances (not a job interview), it is a great opener (for counselling interviews in a highly non-directed setting), but in a selection interview it is very stretching and possibly threatening for a candidate. Some possible reasons why you're asked this question include:

- The interviewer is behind with paperwork and hasn't had a chance to review your CV properly.
- It's a very general opener encouraging you to give a (brief) overview of your background.
- It's a poorly worded question seeking evidence of personality.
- It's a deliberately broad question just to see what you will come up with.

Sometimes the interviewer will be far more specific: '*Tell me about your career, starting with school, and progressing through the jobs that you have held. Include any accomplishments, and bring me up to the present.*' Even in this scenario you've got to remember to keep things brief. To know how to respond is important and **to do so in two minutes or less is essential**. Otherwise you lose the interviewer, who begins to think about other things. More than two minutes increases the possibility of either boring interviewers or losing their attention.

Take the time before the meeting to plan a short script that you prepare precisely for such occasions. Here are some sample answers for different scenarios:

If you are re-entering the job market after a time away:
'*I have experience in both the not-for-profit and the business sectors, primarily on a project basis. I've been away from salaried positions during the past few years to focus on my family, but even so I have been involved in a number of community-based projects that have enhanced my business skills and given me a good range of contacts.*'

For a simple job change – no career change, no market re-entry:
'*After starting a career with [name of organization] as a management trainee and rising up the career ladder there, I accepted an offer from ____ to work in their ____ division. I am now looking for a position with you because of their decision to relocate.*'

For a career change:

'After graduating from XYZ University with an engineering degree, I accepted a position with ABC to work for their _____ division. After five years of increased responsibility on a variety of projects, I was recruited for DEF to be part of their new division specializing in _____. Now I am here because, as you may know, they have reconsidered their commitment to this area and have shut down that activity.'

Practise your response until you are comfortable with an answer that takes about two minutes. After you give your answer, be quiet and wait for a response.

Q31   Describe the best boss you ever had.

When preparing yourself for this meeting and the job search, consider whom you most enjoyed working for as a boss. On a sheet of paper describe the qualities which that person possessed that affected his or her ability to be effective with you and the other members of the team. While you are at it, describe the qualities of the worst person you ever worked for. Compare your qualities lists for both and see what separates them. It is likely that your best boss's abilities to deal with people were linked with his or her ability to get the job done – namely to be sensitive to the needs and personalities of people.

When the question is asked at your meeting, you are then ready to briefly describe the situation and speak genuinely about the boss. If you have not thought about it before the meeting, you have to pause while you reflect on who your best boss was and then consider what to say before saying it. This is a tough task given the circumstances and pressures of a job interview. Again, if the qualities and type of management style mirror that which you feel the organization aspires to attract, you have scored major points.

Be prepared, of course, for the mirror question about the worst boss you've ever had. If you are asked this question it's better to talk about the situation than the person: '*We were all working under a great deal of pressure and against tight schedules, so it wasn't surprising that he didn't have much time to explain objectives.*'

Q32 Who's the most difficult manager you've ever had to deal with?

Looking at teams often links into the way you respond to managers. This is a danger area – generally you don't want to disclose details about poor relationships with past managers. It's probably best to indicate that you've got on pretty well with all managers in the past, but then talk about difficulties which you were able to handle.

'*I've only had difficulties with one manager, and they were minor ones. Essentially she wasn't too good at delegating – which ultimately made life much harder for her. Gradually however I persuaded her to let me take over a project of my own without day-to-day supervision.*'

Your examples can fairly safely include managers who stray outside operational norms, e.g.:

- Never allowed a typographical error.
- Set impossible deadlines all the time.
- Needed to make all the decisions.
- Trusted no one to take responsibility for anything.
- Would never delegate.
- Delegated problems without the resources to handle them.

But don't criticize a manager for behaviour that would be considered par for the course, e.g. '*My last manager pushed people really hard and was very strict on reaching targets.*'

When answering, make sure the **difficulty is obvious and simple to describe, as well as likely to generate agreement from the interviewer.** Don't criticize a past boss for an attitude that the interviewer may share, such as a rigorous 'clean desk' policy.

Q33 What kind of person would manage you best?

You might also be asked a question about your ideal manager. Again, don't offer a very narrow picture, but do indicate that you are comfortable working with a variety of styles. If you say that you like straightforward, open people who set clear objectives and give feedback when it's necessary, very few organizations will own up to having managers who are not like that! Describe a person in a way that in fact reflects your own flexibility:

'My ideal manager would be a good communicator who enhances the productivity of the team by building on the strengths of team members.'

Q34 How do you like to be managed?

Your answer should, in general, suggest that you're pretty easy to manage. Therefore the answer to this question needs to (a) show that you are aware of areas of potential difficulty in management relationships, and (b) indicate that you will respond well to supervision, but you don't need to be micromanaged.

'I don't need to be told things twice. Give me a job to do with clear objectives, and I'm happy to get on with it, just checking back with my manager if I hit a major problem. If I have to go to my manager I try to take solutions rather than just problems.'

Q35 What personal characteristics do you think will be needed to be a success in this position?

From the work you have already completed as part of your **Personal Worksheet** and **On the Job EQ**, this should not be a difficult question to address at the interview. Review the list thoroughly before the meeting because you want to be sure you do not take this topic for granted. Persistence, loyalty, strong work ethic, strong communication skills, results orientation, team player, insatiable curiosity – these are among the characteristics that may be included and certainly could be used for starters. Have at your fingertips strong evidence of times when you displayed these qualities.

Again, make sure that the examples you put forward are a good match to the organization or team – pay careful attention to personality aspects described in documents outlining the job.

Q36 Do you prefer delegation or 'hands-on' control?

This is a good question because there is **no right or wrong answer**. The interviewer is trying to **determine the 'fit' of your approach** to work with the environment. If you are a natural delegator, you will need to build a mutual feeling of trust in your subordinates. 'Hands-on' control demands a different approach by you and by each subordinate. This question should be directly and openly answered because, if the situation requires a real delegating manager and you happen to be real 'hands-on', the fit is not a good one unless you are really flexible. Even then the chances are that, even if you are hired, when the pressure mounts you will revert to your old management style – and that could spell disaster.

Q37 What kind of people do you like to work with? What do you feel is the easiest type of person to deal with? The most difficult?

These three relationship questions seek to determine what makes for an easy personal interaction for you. Do you prefer the direct, hands-on approach, or do you look instead for the person who just gives you enormous autonomy? To be prepared for any of these questions, determine whom:

■ You are best able to deal with.
■ You have had to deal with organizationally, and are best to work for and with.
■ You have had the greatest difficulty working with.

To take a comprehensive approach and to be sure you are identifying every possible type of person you have had to interact with at work, think up, down and at the same level. If you are hit with any of these questions, be prepared to answer all three.

'Who is the most difficult person to work with?' is not as easy to deal with as the other two questions. But do not become worried or defensive because this is really a gift question. Try to identify annoying characteristics that are universally abhorred:

■ The person who refuses to stay when asked to help to solve a problem.
■ Fellow workers who work at a pace that just barely keeps them employed.
■ Someone who tries to avoid responsibility for deadlines.

If you agree that one or more of these types are the worst, then you have your answer.

*Q38 What are your strengths? What are your weaknesses?

Sometimes interviewers will even give you a specific number of strengths and weaknesses they want to hear about. Take this opportunity to share with the interviewer your strong points, particularly those qualities that are relevant for the position at hand and also important to you. Loyalty, a strong work ethic, good interpersonal and communications skills, a project and results orientation are all personal characteristics that interviewers love to hear. Be prepared to give situations that exemplify one or more of your personal characteristics.

The question about weaknesses usually travels on the heels of a question about strengths. Do not be as open with your weaknesses as with your strong points. Try to identify qualities (or their lack) that are not damaging to the position being discussed, or weaknesses that are actually strengths:

'I'm sometimes criticized for being a workaholic.'

'I am impatient with others who display no sense of urgency.'

'People tell me I'm too painstaking at times – but someone's got to check that things are right.'

Q39 If I spoke to your current/former boss, what would he or she say are your greatest strengths/your greatest weaknesses?

Back to personal strengths and weaknesses, but with a different spin. As to weaknesses, you can't say, *'My boss would say that he/she has a difficult time identifying any weaknesses in my current position.'* If you do, you have avoided the question successfully but offered an unrealistic-sounding answer. Best to point out something that you learned or overcame that used to be a weakness: '*When I started the job she would have said that I didn't delegate too well and took most tasks on myself. However I learned to really take advantage of the strengths of my team.*' Alternatively: '*I used to be a worker who always wanted to complete every project perfectly. I have learned to determine a quality standard and be realistic about its importance in the context of the variety of tasks and projects I am responsible for.*'

Q40 What do you think of your current/former boss?

In preparation for this answer, remember that far more people leave jobs because of their boss than because of the job or the organization.

Even though the question has been raised, **caution, not candour, is the rule.** Keep focused on the reason for the question: The interviewer is trying to work out how well you will get on with one or more particular bosses. **This is a direct assessment question to determine if there is a fit between you and a specific business relationship.** Your choice of words when discussing your boss gives the interviewer a chance to assess your ability and under what conditions of leadership you can function most effectively.

It is important that you begin with positives. No matter how bad you (and perhaps countless others) perceived the person to be, this is not the time to disclose your strong negative feelings. At the same time do not overpraise. By giving an assessment that is weighted toward the positive but balanced, you are demonstrating to the interviewer the depth you have in assessing the performance of others and your ability to work with others by playing to strengths and supporting weaknesses.

A sample answer then will go like this:

'I respected my boss because she had a tough job due to all the changes going on organizationally and in the marketplace – yet she was able to get the work done. In spite of all this, she was effective because she balanced the needs of the team with those demanded by her own boss so that she absorbed a lot of the pressure herself and her team understood what she was doing. At times she had difficulty balancing these various needs and it would occasionally show because she would cut corners and quality would suffer.'

Let us consider a worst-case boss. For a truly terrible boss for whom you had no respect and who was miserable as a person, you might consider:

'My boss was one of the most challenging persons I have had the opportunity to work for anywhere in my career so far. He had a lot going on personally that made his working situation a particularly difficult one. Because of the internal situation, he seemed driven by the need to concentrate on the task aspects of his responsibilities and as a result the "people needs" were given less than the needed attention. We had a lot of company-induced turnover as a result that led to more challenges for him and added to the stress of the situation for him. However, I learned to consider my boss as my most demanding "customer", and that worked pretty well.'

Q41 What aspects of your last position did you dislike?

(This could also, of course, be a question about your present job.) This is a great question for both you and the interviewer. For you, it's a gift (provided you are prepared) because it affords you the opportunity to demonstrate how you perceive work. Just be careful to stay focused and brief. Go back to the exercise in **Chapter 2, Job History Worksheet** and see what items you can highlight. Obviously, the aspects you like least are what have brought you to this interview and the features you like best are those that have kept you at that job up to now. Select features on your least-liked list that are not identifiable or not important in the new organization, and features that will be fixed if you are offered the new job: '*I really don't enjoy working in telesales – I'd much rather be seeing customers face to face*'.

Q42 Describe a recent team you worked in. How did the team work?

This is an open-ended question to determine the characteristics and dynamics of teams you have worked within. Give an overview of why the team was formed, how big it was, and the way the team worked. Mention in particular if the team was multi-disciplinary or included a mix in terms of seniority. Communicate, briefly, whatever is appropriate to assist the interviewer to determine the kind of group you have experience working with. Go on to characterize the group in terms of the work situation – tight-knit, high work ethic, good-natured but serious about work – so that the interviewer is able to complete the picture and to compare it to the one you would be dealing with if a job were offered to you.

*Q43 What do you normally contribute to a team?

Here you need to be aware of the different ways that people contribute to teams. Don't be satisfied with the generalized term 'team player'. When we talk about 'team players' most people mean those who are naturally extrovert and who display leadership characteristics. However there are many different ways that people can contribute to teams, e.g.:

■ **Team Leader** – the person who sets targets and boundaries.

- **Team Coach** – the person who gets a great performance out of others.
- **Team Builder** – the person who makes sure that other members of the team get on with each other.
- **Idea Builder** – the person who is good at generating new ideas.
- **Idea Developer** – the person who is good at building on other people's ideas.
- **Safe Pair of Hands** – the person who makes sure things get done and projects are completed on time.

Q44 Let me describe the team you would be joining if we appointed you. How would you fit in?

The employer is asking you to consider the team environment of the workplace. You want to address this question whether or not the question is asked by the interviewer; you should be asking it of yourself. Try to work out the characteristics of the team you hope to be joining. Can you see yourself working here? What will you bring to the party? What problems would you anticipate?

Use terms to describe your role in the team. Use terms which the recruiter understands. You might want to use the terminology from Belbin Team Types (for further details see www.belbin.com). Alternatively, use the kind of terms set out above, or other recognizable terms such as facilitator, synthesizer, enabler, consensus builder, supporter. Use whatever term is an accurate, brief description of the role you played as a member of the team.

The answer requires you to possess a realistic understanding of the position and the team. An example of a strong but brief answer is:

'In teams I tend to be good at getting people to reach a consensus. A good example is the recent project where we had to investigate

centralized accounting. The team was in danger of collecting too much information and never coming to any conclusions. The critical step was for the team to agree to my suggestion that we agree a deadline for finishing our research and also agree a set of criteria to help us decide on our recommendations.'

Q45   What would be your ideal team?

Be honest with yourself in your preparation for the interview. Be ready to answer this question, but remember that the reason for asking the question is to determine whether you are compatible with the team that you would be joining if a job offer is extended. There are two approaches to this question.

1. If the employer has already shared with you his or her perceptions of the major characteristics of the team, then you need to determine which of those elements are most compatible with yours. By identifying them, you can demonstrate a good fit.
2. If the interviewer has not disclosed any characteristics of the team, take a positive approach and, if it is perceived to be appropriate, that is fine. Here is an example:

   'My ideal team has a strong work ethic but also a sense of fun. Ideally, each of the participants will have a real commitment to a high-quality product – plus a respect for each other's ideas and input. I believe this kind of team performs with very little guidance and direction. If a problem arises, it is addressed and solved by the group itself.'

Q46   Have you ever had to sack somebody – or make redundancies? How did you handle it?

Expect this question if you have disclosed on your CV that you have managerial experience. It may be that you've never had to dismiss someone, or make redundancies. What you may need to show, however, is whether you are capable of dismissing a member of staff if it comes to it. If you have never fired an employee, say so. If you were involved, regardless of the level, but not the decision-maker, say you were part of the process and leave it at that.

The easiest answer is an affirmative one with no conditions or hedging. If you have done it, say so and stop. 'Letting people go' is one of the most difficult tasks that a manager has to deal with for several reasons. You may have to make redundancies because of restructuring or downsizing. Expressing sympathy with those whose jobs were lost and acknowledging the psychological and economic concerns behind the decision shows that you do not take these tasks lightly. Alternatively, you may need to dismiss a member of staff due to the performance. Here it's best to be as objective and professional as you can – and under no circumstances should you indicate that the decision was personal.

'As a manager, I have had to make redundancies. More often than not the writing was already on the wall, but in a few cases the employee was genuinely shocked. Fortunately, a generous severance package and outplacement counselling were on offer. The important thing was to provide support and encouragement for those who stayed.'

'Since I was in charge of the unit, I was responsible for the annual review of staff members. Several times I had to put employees on warnings for poor performance and then follow up with termination. In one case I was able to get the employee transferred to another area more suited to his skills.'

Q47 In what ways are you creative?

Every job demands some creativity. If you are a copywriter in an advertising agency you need to draw upon that creativity obviously, but remember there are many different kinds of creativity. You might feel that if you are working in a book-keeping department, creativity is not highly valued – this may be true if you are seeking a job where you can express yourself artistically, but on the other hand you may have an inventive way of organizing data or designing spreadsheets. It might be worth prefacing your answer with a question about what kind of creativity is seen to be appropriate for this job. **Work out what kind of creativity is required, and offer matching examples from your experience.**

'Most people don't think that purchasing is a creative role, but in fact it's about constantly reinventing the relationship with suppliers, and coming up with some fairly innovative solutions to make them work.'

Q48 How would you describe your own personality?

Review the first section of the **Personal Worksheet** that you completed earlier to choose the adjectives that are 'you'. Do not be afraid to use a dictionary or thesaurus to be absolutely certain about various shades of meaning.

Gregarious	Relaxed
Open to new ideas	Deadline-driven
Innovator	Focused
Listener	Attentive
Attention to detail	Sensitive
Work-oriented	Empathetic
Task driven	Aggressive/assertive
Planner	Loyal
People driver	Punctual
Spontaneous	Control-oriented
Self-motivated	Team leader
High energy	Completer-finisher

Self-starter
Cautious

Analytical
Questioning

There is no reason to do this alone. Ask friends, family and business associates what words could be used to describe you. In many cases, friends are delighted to help with your job search in any capacity. Ask yourself what kind of personality is needed to fill the position and cite the characteristics that support your candidacy.

When the Spotlight is on 'You'

- **Do not contradict yourself**. Let your 'non-verbal' message match your sales pitch; act confidently and highlight your past successes and current skills.
- **Do not let your guard down** for questions you may think are 'soft' or 'informal'. Everything is part of the interview.
- **Be prepared** with crisp, focused responses. Write down short, upbeat responses – don't memorize them word for word, but have a pretty clear idea about what you are going to say.
- **Sell your interpersonal skills**. Show how easy and great you would be to work with/for.
- **Enlist help** with your self-analysis; identify your 'best' and 'worst' points. Learn how to present weaknesses that don't really put you in a bad light.
- **Continue to grow personally and professionally**. Read, take classes, meet with fellow professionals, network, or attend seminars. Keep sharp and current.
- **Form a 'success team'** of several trusted friends (not necessarily co-workers) to meet periodically to discuss career strategies.

8

Your Motivation and Career Aspirations

WHAT YOU WANT TO ACHIEVE

Motivation and Career Change

Many of the questions you will be asked will be related to one aspect of personality – what has motivated you throughout your career? These questions will look at your past choices in order to try to work out how well you will be motivated if you get the present job. They may also look at the factors that make a job interesting for you and keep you interested – the key to retention.

Q49   What has been the high point of your career?

This is a double-edged question. If you talk glowingly about a past job, the interviewer may feel that the rest of your career is downhill; if you have already done your best work, only less than that is left. On the other hand, having no high point demonstrates a lack of motivation. A good answers links both past and future:

'I think the role I most enjoyed was working as an account executive in a PR company. However, as enjoyable as the job was, it didn't really give me an opportunity to work with top decision-makers. This role, however...'

Q50 How do you feel about looking for another job?

This question will unearth something about your emotional stability. How do you feel about the ups and downs of looking for a job? How do you cope with rejection? Take a positive, upbeat approach: 'Looking for another job is an opportunity' or 'I don't have to look for another job. I do it so that I can continue to grow professionally.' What the interviewer hopes to hear is that you take charge of your own destiny. You are not looking because you have little or no choice. You need to demonstrate that you are in control and feeling positive about change.

Q51 Tell me about your job search.

This stress-building question can easily intimidate you if you have not prepared. This is definitely a question calling for a matching **Presentation Statement** (see **Chapter 6**). Be consistent with any other information furnished on your application or CV, but be upbeat. If you drone on about how difficult and depressing your job search has been you may win sympathy but you won't get a job offer because you are (a) negative and (b) unsuccessful.

If obviously there has been some length of time since your last job and this has been an undesirable fact of life for you, try to put a positive spin even in the direst of circumstances. Most employers do not want to be faced with a desperate applicant. So try your best to avoid looking like one. Reasons for an extended job search may include:

- '*Searching for the right opportunity.*' You have been looking for *the* job, not *a* job.
- '*Trying to find a real career opportunity with the right organization.*' You have had offers but for one reason or another

you preferred to continue the search. If you take this tack, be ready to support it with concrete examples of job offers that you passed up. Do not make the list too long, even if true; two or three examples should always suffice.

■ *'Personal matters to deal with.'* As more and more people are living longer, the working population is more frequently placed in a position of providing assistance to those older than themselves as well as to children. This is true not only for immediate family but for other relatives, neighbours and friends (including friends of parents) as well. State that you had matters to attend to and, rather than give less than your full attention to your job search, you felt it more appropriate to solve the immediate problem and then give all your energies to the search, which you are now doing.

■ *'Completing my education.'* Have you missed out on educational opportunities in the past for whatever reason (finances, family, other commitments, such as an obligation to take responsibility for managing the family's business)? Currently more and more employers feel that the things you studied over 10 years ago are not too relevant, and that what matters is *continuous professional development.* Attending courses shows you are more likely to be current with the latest thinking in your industry. Whether the courses are job-related (especially directly) or not, you are perceived as a person interested in personal growth as an ongoing commitment and one who becomes excited by the thrill of the new.

■ *'I've been doing some consultancy work.'* This is an over-used excuse. Recruiters are always talking about all the out-of-work people who claim they have been consulting while searching for a job. Just as we mentioned with educational pursuits, if this is the route you pursue, make sure you have a complete story because interviewers will probe this easily. Be ready to talk about client profiles, perhaps disclosing industry, size, employee numbers, revenues, and/or number of work locations. You don't have to disclose the client's name. By creating a little mystery you are stealing the interviewer's opportunity to evaluate the prestige of your client and to peg you in terms of professional stature. Also, if the interviewer is interested, be ready with a brief summary (very focused and very brief) of the nature of the engagement, including a comment about the result.

■ '*I am attempting a change in career.*' If you mean it, then be prepared to talk about ways you have seriously invested in the process of career exploration. You must anticipate booby traps. Is the job or organization you are meeting with consistent with the new career? What activities have you pursued to quickly build up your knowledge in this new area? If you are contemplating a career change, don't consider yourself odd or an exception. Charles Handy in *The Age of Unreason* suggested that we now expect to make at least three career changes in our lifetimes. John Lees' *How To Get The Perfect Promotion* includes research that indicates that some people in the UK now expect to change career no less than five times in total. Career change that is made as an active choice rather than an act of desperation indicates you are prepared to take control of your life.

■ '*You called me. I was not looking.*' This is a strong response when you have been recruited by a headhunter. This answer puts interviewers on the defensive perhaps because they were not aware of it (and your question now has them weakened because of their lack of information).

Even if you have been looking for a job for a year or more without success, move on from this topic quickly. Employers get worried by individuals who, despite an active and thorough job-search, don't get job offers. In the interview focus on the job, not your difficulties finding it.

*Q52 Why do you want to leave your present job?

Prepare for this question, because it's very predictable and it's really important.

Your answer should focus on positive reasons for change, and should avoid criticism, implied or explicit, about the organization. Do not whine that they would not promote you (or give you an increase, a corner office, a higher commission rate). Don't talk about difficult relationships, and certainly don't talk about how you fell out with your boss.

Essentially, what your answer should be saying is that you have a strong but positive motivation to move on. Try to say something positive about your last or current employer. Criticizing employers tends to communicate 'troublemaker'. Rehearse a short, upbeat statement, such as:

- *'I've learned what I can in the role.'*
- *'I've been through the process several times and it's time to do something new.'*
- *I've really enjoyed the job, but I'm looking for a new challenge.'*

If you are currently employed, the most important thing is not to demonstrate disloyalty to the company that is still paying your salary. Don't criticize the organization or your colleagues, because if you do the interviewer will have a mental picture of you saying exactly the same things in the new role. You can generate a positive answer by referring to much more neutral ideas, e.g.:

- **Industry-wide changes**. *'New technology is making the organization's product obsolete.' 'Manufacturing is going off-shore.'*
- **Organizational circumstances**. *'The organization is restructuring... going out of business... has been acquired/ merged/spun off...'*
- **Geographical relocation**. *'The organization is leaving the area.' 'My spouse/partner is moving jobs.'*

■ **Personal concerns**. '*Organizationally I have gone as far as I could. The person above me is just two years older and there is nowhere else for her to go at this time.*' Although you can talk about reaching the end of your learning curve (in other words, you can now do the job with minimum input and it's no longer stretching you) be careful that your message doesn't sound like '**I've learned all there is to know about the job**'. That contains a strong hint of arrogance. If that is what interviewers hear (whether that is an accurate reading of your comments or not), they may 'hear' that you are bigger than the job, or that 'if you hire me, you will have a problem because if you don't keep offering me learning opportunities, I will look elsewhere.'

Q53   Why did you leave your last position?

Be consistent with your answer. Consider reasons you may have included in your cover letter, other conversations with recruiters, and anything your referees might say if asked. If you are still employed or on speaking terms with your former employer, it is best **to have the same story for why you are no longer employed in case of reference checks**. It is a small world, and it is not a difficult task to corroborate your account.

What matters almost as much as the specific reason to this question is the tone and non-verbal gestures you use while giving your answer. You need to be comfortable and confident with the answer that you give, regardless of what you say. If you have been fired for whatever reason, tell the truth but speak cautiously. **Never lie, but remember you have control over what you say and how you say it.** Interviewers to whom you are telling your tale were not there, and they probably do not have a familiarity or understanding of the circumstances you are describing. They will retain negative information about you for a long time. You can certainly put a positive spin on any situation by describing how you learned from this development in your professional life.

Disputes, Legal or Otherwise

It's nearly always unwise to mention disputes with previous employers – even if you're just negotiating the final details of a redundancy package. Employers generally react very badly to staff who are taking their previous employer to court or to an industrial tribunal. Keep off the subject as far as possible, and if it is raised, deal with it as simply and quickly as you can: '*I had to take legal advice to resolve the situation, but it's all sorted out now.*'

Don't use the interview as an opportunity to sound off about your gripes against a former boss or employer. Telling the interviewer how badly you were treated may get you sympathy, but you can easily be tainted with the label of either 'troublemaker' or 'victim', neither of which encourages an appointment decision.

Q54 Had you thought of leaving your current/past position before? If so, what held you there?

Good interviewers ask this question. They are attempting to learn your motivation and your ability to consider a course of action and then take it. You should be prepared to talk in a balanced way about how you weighed up a past career decision. Since you stayed in the organization, clearly your answer needs to suggest that you made the right decision:

'*I was approached by a company that were interested in getting me to set up a new sales branch. However at that time we were in the middle of a really important project and I wanted to see it through to the end.*'

Q55 How will you react if your present employer makes a counter-offer?

This question may come up if you are currently in a job, and you shouldn't be surprised by it. Some recruiters will even ask you how you will phrase your resignation letter. The reason is that a proportion of candidates who get to job offer stage turn down the job because they are just not ready to move. Some of them are just 'fishing' to see what they are worth in the marketplace. They review their situation and decide it's more comfortable to stay. Or their employer makes a counter-offer.

It's quite common that when a worker accepts a job offer and tries to resign, the original employer tries to fix the problem by making a counter-offer: 'We'll match that salary offer' or 'We'll promote you'. There is a theory widely held in the recruitment industry in both the UK and US that anyone who accepts a counter-offer from their current employer moves on anyway within 18 months. The reasons? Usually a counter-offer only gets the money issues right, and doesn't deal with the underlying problems.

Q56 How long have you been looking for a job?

Don't respond to any question about your job search by talking about how difficult the marketplace is, and how depressing it feels to get rejection letters. A recruiter isn't interested, but may wonder why so many other organizations have said 'no'. Some people feel that the longer you have been looking for a job, the weaker you appear to interviewers because they will wonder why it is taking so long. Worse is the perception that, if no one is interested in hiring you, what are they doing spending time with you?

In fact, it's all about how you present your answer. If you have been looking for a while and you want to admit it, then give it a positive spin. 'I've been looking for a while because I don't want to take the first thing that comes along – I want to make the right career move' or 'I don't want A job, I want the RIGHT job'. You have had offers, but they haven't been right. If you take this route, be really ready to discuss the rejected offers because it is such an obvious opener that begs for the 'next' question. Make your answers show how clear you are about the elements that make an ideal job (which will of course match you to this job). Best to be brief, honest, and don't linger:

'I was made redundant last June. The first three months were tied up taking a refresher course in accounting. Since then I've focused on finding not just a job, but the right job for me.'

Q57 What career options do you have at this moment?

To share one or more alternatives here (in addition to the one you are discussing with the interviewer) is to risk the inter- viewer's perception either that you are not that interested in the position being discussed or that you are unfocused. Remember: **the job you are being interviewed for is the most important job in the world to you, right now.**

There is an exception: Suppose you are beginning your career and meeting a recruiter from an organization that offers several career options at entry level. In such a case, you can mention more than one option to keep your options open in case one track is over-subscribed. For example, the person with a degree in finance and global management may consid- er either a domestic investment banking position or one in the international division. If that is shared with anyone in the organization, remember to stay consistent with that approach throughout the interview process in the organization. With luck, both groups may fight for you and the offer taken should not limit your going forward. Consider recruitment interviews as networking opportunities, and you should try to maintain those contacts as you move through the organization in your chosen career track.

When possible, open up the idea that you have many different facets:

'In my career in sales I have worked in both new business development and managing existing accounts. I enjoy both challenges – winning new clients and keeping existing ones.'

Q58 What do you look for in a job?

Offer a brief statement that links your personal goals with those of the organization. It's often best to put the organization's needs first in your list: '*I am looking for a company that really wants to offer added value to customers, and a role in that organization where I can make a real difference to staff attitudes and behaviours.*' You may also consider the best job you ever had (see below) to confirm your thoughts on this question before the meeting. Of course, it is advantage to have a positive correlation between this response and the job that the organization has open is an advantage.

Q59 Describe the best job you ever had.

By preparing for this question ahead of time, you avoid the need to consider the question on the spot, do a quick sort to find the job, and then scramble mentally to put some coherent words together. This question may not be dissimilar from the previous question '**What do you look for in a job?**' because, by considering the best job you ever had, you probably identify specifics that help you decide what you are looking for in a job. Do not make your 'best' job too dissimilar from the one for which you are being considered. What you are essentially doing is offering a 'recipe' for job success that should be fairly close to the position on offer.

Q60 Describe a major goal you have recently set for yourself.

Select a meaningful project that is either personal or professional in nature. 'Complete my education' is one. 'Find the right job' is another. The second is preferable because it brings the discussion back to the topic you are there to discuss – **a job for you in this specific organization.** To portray this as a major goal leaves no doubt about the fact one more time that you are very serious about a career and a job with the organization. This is a statement that does not hurt no matter how often you make it, as long as you don't sound desperate or sorry for yourself.

Q61 How do you feel about your career progress to date?

Beware this doesn't lead you into a wistful answer about the 'road not taken'. Remember that you are not dealing with a therapist but a job interviewer. It's generally less distracting to say something like, *'I'm happy with my career so far'*. Then, if you need to think of something you might have done differently, talk about something that would have made your arrival at your current point swifter: *'I only wish that I had applied to this organization when I was starting.'*

You can discuss the ups and downs of your career candidly with a friend or a careers coach, but take care how you answer this question in an interview. The best tack is to demonstrate satisfaction to a point, and that point is the reason for deciding to move on in this direction now:

'I've really enjoyed working in Human Resources, and I've had the chance to do a lot of fascinating jobs. However I've come to realize that I actually enjoy making a direct contribution to the bottom line of a business, which is why I am now actively seeking a sales role.'

Q62 How do you define success?

This is a question about your motivation that should be considered before the meeting, not so much for the interviewer's sake as for your own. In the meeting however, realize that the person asking the question is asking it in an organizational – not a career counselling – context. You may consider **linking recognition to meaningful contribution** as an answer: 'I define success as being well rewarded for achieving an organization's critical objectives.' Be prepared for a probing question about times when you have done this in the past.

Q63 If you could, what would you change about this position?

You may have an interviewer who is after some free consultancy input, or someone who wants to see if you are already changing things before the job is even offered. Before the job offer it's best to say, *'Until I am actually in the position and see what works and what doesn't, I would be hard pressed to make any recommendations.'* When you have a job offer, however, you have some limited leverage in persuading an organization to change the job description to match your strengths.

Q64 What do you like most about this position? What do you like least about this position?

This question usually has two parts, which come one at a time. The set-up comes with asking what you like best first because it is the easier of the two. (If you cannot think of any positives, why are you still there?) To answer what you like the most, identify two or three major job elements or characteristics that really are the essence of the job:

■ *'I like the amount of time that will be devoted to clients.'*

■ *'I particularly like the problem solving elements of the position.'*
■ *'The team that I would work with looks terrific.'*

When being positioned to identify the least attractive aspects of the position, try to avoid the question by saying, '*I can't think of anything that I dislike about the position.*' Or, '*It sounds just like I had hoped it would be.*' Appear confident and knowledgeable about the position. Then try to share something that the interviewer has already mentioned about it so that you are an empathizing, perceptive and good listener. Or come up with an obvious, minor drawback:

'The only thing that will make the position a difficult one is the fact that you're operating on a split site, but I'm sure you already have many ways of dealing with that problem.'

Don't use this question as a prompt to complain about the salary or terms and conditions: discussing related problems or dislikes at this point can screen you out.

Q65 What are your long-term goals?

Be practical and realistic. Demonstrate that you are a person with a future orientation: 'I would like to continue to make a real contribution to the organization's success while growing professionally'. Don't be too specific about salary or job levels you'd like to attain – they may not be possible here, and the interviewer may feel you are after his or her job!

Q66 What will you do if this position is not offered to you?

Treat this question seriously. Act disappointed but professional:

'Naturally I'd be disappointed because I think my background is a good match for what you're looking for. Since I am very impressed

with this organization, I would ask for some feedback and whether I could be considered for other similar positions in the future.'

*Q67   Where do you hope to be in five years' time?

This is one of those standard questions that someone thought up years ago and for some reason it has continued to grow in popularity. It is not a bad question because it is open-ended with a time line. The applicant is expected to provide a realistic answer that portrays neither a lust for power ('I want to be your boss') nor a passive lack of focus and ambition ('I want to win the lottery'). Instead, the candidate is expected to show bridled ambition (except in a few organizations that want to see a 'killer' attitude):

'I'd hope to still be with this organization, in a position of increased responsibility where I will be able to continue my professional growth while making an ongoing contribution to the organization's success.'

Q68   Would you consider taking unpaid work?

This question is generally only asked by charities or if the interviewee has just left the education system and is desperate for work experience. Some employers offer what are called in the USA 'internships' – i.e. unpaid positions which offer a valuable chance of gaining work experience. Sometimes the situation is one of a start-up company low in funds. Consider whether it enhances your value to a potential employer to accept a non-paying job in the hope of getting a paying one later. Be careful because frequently a perception goes with your salary level, bluntly stated as, 'You get what you pay for.'

Keep in mind also that the time you spend in work is time not spent looking for a job. There is a trade-off of your time and attendant costs in working for 'free' with the ability of getting your foot in the door and receiving on-the-job training. To show interest in the organization but discourage your being thought of as free labour, try saying:

'I would jump at the chance to work here, but unfortunately my financial situation means that I would be distracted by any other paid job offers that came along.'

Here again, focusing on the size of the employer's needs may unlock the coffers. If you really decide it's helpful to take unpaid work, make sure there is some kind of a 'trade off' – in other words, you are getting significant learning opportunities, useful work experience, feedback, and a good reference. Always seek something in return – your contribution will be valued more.

Q69 Would you like to have [your prospective manager]'s job?

Be diplomatic. *'I need to concentrate on the position I am being considered for at this time. That will be more than enough to occupy my efforts for quite a while to come.'*

Q70 It would seem that you don't really have the experience/qualifications for this post. What do you say to that?

Interviewers may be letting you know that they have already written you off and they may or may not be giving you one last shot at convincing them otherwise. This question cries out, 'You had better show me or else!'. Additionally, it may display the true feeling of the interviewer that says, 'The clock is ticking and I am running out of patience.'

On the other hand, the interviewer may feel that qualifications are not an issue but want to hear it from you. ('Let me be a devil's advocate for a moment ...') Either way, treat the question as one that addresses **standards**. Very few jobs require either qualifications or experience in absolute terms – and there are always ways in, around, or under such requirements. The important thing is to demonstrate that (a) your experience makes up for your lack of qualifications, or (b) the quality of your experience is more important than the length of service.

You need to strike a balance between agreeing with the person's concerns on the surface and providing a convincing answer that serves to neutralize the concern expressed. One approach may be to start with, '*I certainly appreciate your comment and might agree with your concern.*' (Try to avoid using 'but' here.) '*... I wonder whether you have given attention to ...*'. Avoid using words like 'enough' or 'ample', which may be considered a criticism and may put interviewers on the defensive because they may feel placed in a position of attack. Once this statement is delivered, a strong positive response must follow. The response should give interviewers the opportunity to agree that they had not been aware of something in your experience, at the same time taking some responsibility for having the interviewer initially thinking otherwise.

'*I am not certain whether I stressed my experience in designing websites in my spare time using professional standard software ...*'

In a worst case scenario, when interviewers are being kind and you know that you don't have any of the experience that they want, briefly and directly agree with the interviewer. Then move on to a positive assertion that indicates your potential.

Q71 What would you say if I suggested that you are over-qualified for this position?

This again may be an indication that the interviewer has come to a conclusion. However, the fact that the interviewer is sharing this concern with you gives you a chance to address the problem. Think yourself into the interviewer's shoes. Candidates who are over-qualified may be, in the eyes of a recruiter:

- **A threat** – you will want promotion quickly.
- Making the **wrong choice** – you'll move on quickly.
- Someone who will rapidly become **bored with the job** and demotivated.
- A **know-it-all** who will make your boss's life hell.
- **Desperate** to take any job at any salary.

If it's clear that the job you're looking at will appear to be a demotion, or that you will be much more qualified and/or experienced than others in the same post, don't leave this issue unaddressed.

'Yes, on paper I will be more qualified than others in this department. But the job will allow me to learn a great deal as well. I'm certainly not looking at this job as a soft option.'

Q72 What kind of tasks really get you energized?

If you haven't been talking along these lines just yet, it's time you started. Interviewers begin to pay attention when they hear real energy and enthusiasm in your tone of voice. This, more than anything, conveys what will really motivate you in a job.

Equally, nothing talks you out of a job faster than a tired, listless series of responses that sounds as if everything in life is really rather dull and slightly too much trouble.

Prepare in advance to talk about things at work that give you a buzz:

'A real high point for me was designing our last exhibition stand. I wanted to do something really different, really high-tech – and it worked!'

Q73 If you could choose any organization, where would you go?

This is an opportunity for you to demonstrate the depth of your knowledge and scope of your interest. Remember, in an interview *the present job is the only and most important job.* State simply, *'This is the kind of organization I am looking for because …'.*

Preparation around Motivation Questions

If you can answer these questions for yourself, you'll be far more prepared if questions on this topic area come up during the interview.

■ Not having enough money or being underpaid is a powerful demotivator. How far is **money** a motivator for you? How long does a pay rise improve your performance?

■ So if money is a weak motivator in real terms, **what really motivates you in work**? Look at the key issues that matter once the money issues are fixed: respect from colleagues, a good boss, recognition, status, learning opportunities, the sense of a challenge ….

■ What things tend to **demotivate** you at work? How affected are you by the physical environment (grubby offices, poor location)? How easily are you demotivated by criticism or uncaring colleagues?

■ What could past employers have done to retain you? What can you **negotiate** with your next employer that will improve your job and give rewards to your employer?

■ What kind of work would you do if all jobs paid the same?

For further exploration on the power of motivation, see John Lees' *How To Get A Job You'll Love*.

Education Questions

YOUR KNOW-HOW

Not too long ago the idea of the 'learning organization' took hold of the corporate imagination: a company that has the ability to flex, to adapt, and to both manage and extend its knowledge base. There is also pressure on individuals to keep learning. This might be academic learning, but is more commonly:

- learning new systems, techniques, and principles
- learning about technological developments in your field
- learning about your company, its competitors, and the marketplace
- learning new skills, and improving old ones.

Interviewers are interested in your education in a number of respects. If you qualified recently, they will want to know why you made your educational choices, and how the subjects you chose have assisted your career. If you left the education system some time back, an interviewer will be interested in your continuing professional development – in other words, what you have done to keep your skills and knowledge up to date. This may be demonstrated by training programmes you have attended, study you have undertaken in or out of work, or other kinds of learning opportunities: seminars, conferences, online learning. They seek to determine how professionally skilled and developed you are. How do you learn? And how quickly can you learn a new job?

Reasons to Become a Lifelong Learner

- The **way work is done** is changing rapidly. This year's innovation becomes last year's traditional method.
- **Technology** accelerates at such a pace that it offers radical new ways of working every 6 months or so.
- **Continuing education is seen as more effective** than the traditional 'qualify and then work' approach.
- **Occupations rise and fall**. Not to realize this fact may make the 'professional' perfectly prepared for a job that has become as obsolete as the industry providing it.

To review all that you do 'know' and your educational history, complete the **Education Worksheet** opposite. Do not neglect to list any on-the-job training, seminars or workshops you may have attended, or classes that you may be currently taking or are enrolled in. Which of these you disclose as being relevant to the job opening is certainly under your control.

Knowledge, of course, is not limited to classroom learning; review again the third section (What I Know) of the **Personal Worksheet (Chapter 2)** to remind yourself of 'hidden' knowledge. Look again at all the night classes, distance learning courses and books you read *just to learn things for the sake of learning*.

Consider what skills or types of knowledge are necessary for this position (and for future advancement) and list these on the **On the Job Knowledge** form. Again, if you are applying for a job as an administrative assistant, you may not wish to disclose your shorthand skills if you don't want to perform secretarial work. Write next to each area of know-how how you came by it or where you acquired it. For example, you may have a knowledge of Quicken accounting software because you use it for your personal bank records or you may have learned Spanish in a holiday job. Of particular importance is your honesty in rating the level of proficiency you can offer the organization: find a clear way of communicating the *level* or *standard* of the knowledge. Ways of doing this include:

- What qualifications have you achieved? Are they likely to be recognized and understood by employers?
- If you have knowledge that is acquired through other means, what evidence do you have of the standard of achievement you have obtained?
- What have you done with this knowledge in the past? What problems have you solved?
- How have you applied one area of knowledge to another? For example '*I learned a huge amount about project management in the telecoms industry and discovered that I could usefully apply these disciplines to the field of logistics.*'

Education Worksheet

Provide details for each stage of your academic experience, moving on to training courses you have attended.

Secondary school

Qualifications (and grades):

Other areas of knowledge:

College or university

Qualifications (and grades):

Why did you choose this course of study?:

Special projects or detailed areas of study:

Date graduated (or expected):

Other areas of knowledge:

Future academic plans:

_____

Training courses attended, and on the job training:

_____

Courses you have pursued in your own time:

_____

Other forms of self-organized study (distance learning, online study, textbooks or management books):

On the Job Knowledge

Organization:

Position:

Rate your level of proficiency: 1 = beginner; 2 = intermediate; 3 = experienced; 4 = expert

Skills/knowledge needed for this position	Specific example of when/where you acquired the skill/knowledge	Level

Q74   What have you most enjoyed studying?

Prepare for this and other questions that probe areas of academic study. Be prepared to talk about your study in two ways. First of all, be interesting. If you don't demonstrate enthusiasm for what you have done, the listener certainly won't. Secondly, 'translate' what you have studied into terms that your interviewer will understand. If your dissertation title was *Semiotic Dissonance in 'Paradise Lost'* your interviewer will find little of relevance to the modern workplace. Even if your subject of study doesn't seem to be directly relevant to the job you're after, you should at least be able to talk about skills you used during your studies which are relevant, e.g. researching a subject thoroughly, interviewing people, working in a team.

'What I really enjoyed most in my studies was writing a dissertation on my favourite author. This involved tracking down all kinds of things, and I learned how to organize information and resources for myself. I was even able to persuade the busy international writer to give me an interview – which I think demonstrates tenacity and powers of persuasion!'

*Q75   What have you learned from your studies that will help you in this job?

This is going to be tricky to handle unless you have considered it in advance. Identify one or two key areas in the job, and pick out matching areas of skill or knowledge from your studies (or from activities you undertook while studying), e.g.:

'As organizer of the year's largest charity ball I had my hands pretty full – and I learned a huge amount about booking facilities and entertainment, and how to feed 300 people and make a profit.'

'In my final year I organized a field trip to Norway, using a number of organization and planning skills which I think will be useful in this job'.

Q76 What has a degree in _____ got to do with this job?

You may find interviewers asking this kind of question, sometimes with an incredulous tone of voice. Don't forget it's your job to explain what a qualification is about – in ordinary language. Don't use academic jargon, and do explain it in terms which will be meaningful to the recruiter, bringing out key aspects of your experience while studying (e.g. working in teams, managing projects, working with employers, winning an award).

'I can see how a degree in Zoology may not seem like exactly the right qualification to get me into management consultancy. However, I believe that the function of a degree is really to teach you how to think, how to organize your own learning and manage your time so that you end up with a good degree without being excessively in debt.'

Q77 Why did you study?

Any question that includes the word 'why' is potentially challenging. In all likelihood, the questioner isn't particularly interested in your exact motivation – just the fact that you had a reason. A throw-away *'It seemed a good idea at the time'* is dangerous. Worse still: *'I thought I would enjoy it, but…'.* Be ready with a short positive answer that indicates that you thought about subject choice carefully and you found your studies interesting and useful. Even the suggestion that you chose the wrong subject is disturbing to the interviewer, because it communicates confusion about career objectives. You may be uncertain, but it does your cause no good to share this in a job interview:

'The reason I chose history was to follow a subject I found interesting and to gain a good general degree which would equip me with the intellectual skills for a career in _____.'

'I was really keen to study history, and I firmly believe in the value of studying things that are stimulating and enjoyable. What I want to do now is build on my general abilities as a graduate and move into the field of _____.'

If you are not practicing the field that you studied – for example you studied law but decided not to work as a lawyer – mention specifically that it was not your intention to pursue a profession in that field, otherwise you come across as a failed lawyer.

'Although I did get a law degree, it was never my intention to train as a solicitor. I felt that a legal background combined with my business degree would uniquely prepare me to assume a position in an international organization.'

If you have a solid reason for a change in profession, state it succinctly.

Q78 Why did you attend that particular college/university?

Don't be flippant or snobbish. Interviewers possibly have positive or negative feelings about the university or college and may even have gone there themselves – or a close family member might have. Give the reason that makes the most sense to you and that makes you appear a promising candidate in the interviewer's eyes:

'I saw several articles written by faculty members and was impressed with their command of the subject.'

'It's a great place to be if you're a student – there's so much going on and you get the chance to meet so many interesting people.'

Q79 What have you learned in the last 12 months?

What's the latest thing you've learned? The answer is the essence of this chapter: **Portray yourself as an interested, active, lifelong learner.** Try to avoid putting a time frame on your answer (unless you took a workshop just the other day). This question is a prime example of why it is important to prepare and to complete the various worksheets highlighting your work and education history.

'I've learned a wide number of things. I suppose the course that's most relevant is my recent evening class in Business French. This has hugely widened my vocabulary and given me the chance to try out some live negotiation over the phone with French companies.'

'The job has been too pressured for me to attend any external training programmes, but I have personally led a number of in-house seminars. Teaching your colleagues means you really do have to do your homework ...'

Q80 What professional training courses have you found useful recently?

The key here is to show that you have maintained some form of continuous professional development, and also to talk about training which is relevant to the position on offer. Don't reel off a long list of courses – focus on one or two that are useful here.

'I really enjoyed the team-building course I did this spring. It was well run, and gave me a huge number of insights into leading and motivating a team.'

Q81 How do you learn? What is your learning style?

This nice question gives you the opportunity to talk about yourself without any really right or wrong implications. With the question, interviewers are not, as it might seem, making a note so that, if you are offered the job, you will be given training tailored to your most effective learning style. No, the question seeks to see if you are able to learn quickly and be ready to perform immediately after training. This is, in short, not the place to say, '*I really prefer to study all facets of an issue and become an expert before performing any related activity*'. The only thing that has not been added is the negative implication, '*... and if that takes years ...*'.

Discover something about learning styles (e.g. do you prefer to learn through hands-on, practical applications, or by looking at theory, or by observing and following other people's behaviours?). It is best to present an action-oriented format that underscores that the best way to learn is when you get to perform on the job immediately after any training is completed.

'I tend to be a hands-on learner – I like to put what I learn into practice as quickly as possible.'

'I'm really interested in underlying theories – but I always want to know how they can be used in real situations in the workplace.'

The last element to mention, but not demand, is feedback. You like occasional feedback to ensure that you are putting into action correctly what you have been trained to do. Don't emphasize constant or regular feedback because then the interviewers see that you require constant attention – a problem!

*Q82 How do you keep informed professionally?

The question *assumes that you do keep informed professionally* and that you consider yourself a professional. What do you read on a daily basis? Weekly? Monthly? Quarterly? Depending on your field, a variety of materials are published on all these timescales. Notice the first activity mentioned in response to the question is 'read'. With the proliferation of the television into every area of our lives, TV frequently replaces print media in the development of our intellectual skills, both personally and professionally. You're not expected to read Tolstoy or every management book on the planet, but to have real breadth and depth in your knowledge base.

The art is to match learning resources to the level and nature of the job. If you're interested in becoming a journalist, you should read newspapers. Avidly. If you're seriously interested in working in HR, you should be able to talk about the range of professional journals which cover this field, and as a result be able to talk about:

- Key industry facts and figures.
- Predicted short-term trends in your sector.
- Key people in the industry.
- Major upsets and scandals.
- New theories, applications and ideas that everyone is discussing.

'Even though I have very little time to read, I hardly ever miss an edition of Management Today.'

Q83 What have you learned from the jobs that you have held?

This is an opportunity for you to *summarize your experience from a learning perspective*. Review your **Experience Worksheet** to see what skills and accomplishments who developed from job to job. Mention both the task aspects of work as well as the people relationships, saying directly that your most important relationship is to your boss or immediate supervisor. Try to include the terms 'respect' and 'loyalty' when speaking in an organizational context and discussing its products and/or services. Comment about the value you bring to any job. A sample answer follows:

'I have learned to define what value I add to the organization to ensure that what I am being compensated is worth that and more to the organization. I know that process is a consideration, but results and output are most important. If the organization is going to be competitive, the employees need a customer perspective and to have that, they need to work effectively together. Last, the organization that I work for requires my respect and loyalty.'

Q84 What made you choose to become a lawyer/banker/secretary/engineer?

Avoid all temptations to be flippant even though the question has little bearing on the individual you are now. Before the meeting, recall the motivation you had to become a lawyer, engineer, etc. During the process, determine also why you chose not to go into other fields. Parents and other family members are frequently role models for our professional choices.

The important thing about this question is to demonstrate with your answer that *you were always serious about your career* and that you plan career changes rather than are subject to them.

'I felt originally that I was drawn to banking, and I had five really exciting years in the City. What I eventually realized was that I was much more interested in communicating to people in creative ways, which is why I moved into training...'

*Q85 In what way do you feel you have management potential?

Be realistic about your abilities, especially the higher you rise professionally. Your answer here needs to focus on evidence rather than simple assertions. Focus on times in the past when you have demonstrated behaviours which are appropriate for this organization and role. The ideal answer will cover both potential (*'I'm interested in learning more ...'*) and your experience to date:

'I enjoyed my time as team leader and I believe I developed a number of management skills that I can build upon in this role.'

Q86 Don't you think you would be better suited to a different size/type of company?

What does this question mean? Most probably, the interviewer has either written you off or is testing you. In either instance, *avoid going on the defensive.* Try to take this opportunity to determine what made the interviewer raise the question in the first place.

In one sense, this question is a kind of buying signal. You've indicated the right skills for the job; the interviewer is just concerned that you may be uncomfortable working in this particular kind of organization. Your answer should show how an organization of this size or type is right for you just now:

'I feel now's the time to move into a small company environment where I can gain experience of a number of different functions and be involved in the overall strategy of the business.'

Q87 What important trends do you see in our industry?

This is a serious question that requires focus and preparation, and is a strong indicator of whether you are in fact a lifelong learner. It demands proof that you have done your homework – and it will probably be homework that involves talking to people rather than just desk research. You will relish this kind of question because it gives you a chance to show that *you have done your research and you have real reasons for wanting to join this organization and industry.* Prepare yourself to speak knowledgeably about:

1. The industry – is it rising or falling? How far is it vulnerable to external factors such as overseas competition or automation?
2. What issues are hot in this industry right now? What are people worried or excited about?
3. How does this organization perceive its effectiveness in dealing with these trends and issues?

All this is not something that takes a lifetime to learn but is something that requires a willingness to do research as part of the preparation for any meeting for a job. Go to the **Organization Fact Sheet** to determine if you have enough information to speak intelligently on the industry. Go through relevant publications and keep copies of recent articles of relevance. Try to gain a picture of the way this organization sees its future, and demonstrate that you can be part of it:

'Clearly the biggest trend is the move to online communication. Interactive "magazines" may be the trend of the future and, with my journalist background combined with my recent experience of website design, I am really excited about exploring these options with you.'

Building on your Education and Training

- In what ways could you describe yourself as a perpetual student? Keep an open mind and keep learning.
- **Be aware** of what is happening in your industry.
- **Investigate learning opportunities**. See www.learndirect-advice.co.uk to access the UK's government database of courses and methods of study.
- **Maintain professional relationships**, particularly if you are currently unemployed. Attend seminars and workshops when possible.
- **Undertake voluntary work**, on a limited basis, as a mentor for new businesses, or as a committee member, or as a coach or skills trainer. You might investigate the possibility of teaching around your expertise at your local FE or Adult Education college.
- Think of this **job search as a chance to learn**, to learn about yourself, to learn new skills, and to learn about a range of organizations and disciplines.
- Maintain and follow your curiosity – it's the key to lifelong learning.

10

Prove It!

WHAT HAVE YOU DONE?

It's an old saying in the recruitment industry: **employers buy experience**. Everybody wants to avoid risk in recruitment, and the best bet is someone who has done this job (or something very much like this job) before.

Experience questions are the bread and butter of recruiters, and the most important to deal with for three reasons:

1. Experience questions provide an opportunity for **recall and analysis**, something that all people who are serious about their work should do periodically. We're not doomed to repeat mistakes, but we are at risk of doing so if we don't look back at the work we've done and reflect on what we learned from it.

2. Experience questions are closely related to the **benchmarks for success in a job interview**, and ultimately to the selection decision.

3. These questions are a **great opportunity for you to shine**, for who is a better expert on yourself than you? Just as manufacturers create packaging and develop marketing campaigns to promote their products' latest advantages, you are effectively communicating your own brand values. What makes you distinctive? What is your unique mix of skills, experience, know-how and positive attitude?

Preparing the Evidence

Take time to prepare thoroughly for questions which focus on your experience. The key elements are as follows:

- **Thinking ahead**: By preparing your responses in advance you are taking the interview process seriously. You are also giving yourself an advantage – you will have done your thinking in advance of the interview.
- **Enthusiasm**: Show that you are excited by the work you have already done and look forward to the future.
- **Communication effectiveness**: You are able to speak about your experience in a coherent, organized and interesting way.
- **Focus**: You ensure that the interview centres on your professional experience, not less tangible matters such as personality.
- **Subject matter expertise**: You are the expert on what you have been doing at work.

Preparing for Experience Questions

The art of presenting your experience well at interview is to do your planning work in advance, and not to try to recall useful examples in the interview room itself. Go into an interview well armed with short, clear examples of your work experience. Think in terms of brief achievement stories.

Remember that the perfect interview intends to gain sufficient information about your past experience in order to **try to predict your future workplace performance**. Interviewers are quizzing you in order to gain insights into your professional experiences – the projects and tasks you have handled, your past working relationships, your successes and problems.

Pre-interview preparation is vital because it offers an opportunity to consider work history in the way that a recruiter will be looking at it. Three hours of preparation, including research on the organization and the industry, appears to be a reasonable time to invest for each interview.

A first step is to take a copy of the CV you used to get the interview, and list the relevant points of your professional history. Be prepared, with evidence, to answer questions which probe details in your CV. In particular, be prepared to give additional evidence and examples that are not included in your CV. Using the **Experience Worksheet** below provide all the details (who, what, when, where and why) for your current or most recent job and for all the jobs listed on your CV. Do not omit any part-time or voluntary jobs – although you may not want to list them on your CV, you may need to draw upon them as evidence of skills.

Experience Worksheet

Provide details for each job listed on your CV starting with the current or most recent job.

Employer:

Job title:

Boss's name and job title:

Date started:	Last day of work:
Starting salary:	Current/ending salary:
Starting position:	Current/ending position:

How did you get this job?

Describe most recent duties:

Describe the team you work in, and your contribution to it:

How was your work evaluated?

What evaluation did you last receive?

What did you like best about this job?

What did you like least?

What were your greatest accomplishments in this role?

Skills used?

Major responsibilities?

Promotions/awards/honours?

Why did you leave this position?

Focusing on Critical Incidents

Continue your preparation for these questions by looking at 'critical incidents' that have arisen in your last 12 months at work. The reason for taking the last 12 months is that, by considering the most recent experience, you have good recall of the detail of exactly what happened.

A critical incident will often be one of the most exciting parts of the job because it represents a challenge, or a time when you made a real difference. The situations may require high risk but also offer greater reward. Use the **Critical Incidents Worksheet** opposite to perform this exercise. Do not confine your review to only those incidents where things were all in your favour, but include times when problems ensued or your work was criticized. What did you learn from these 'mistakes'?

Note: this evidence-gathering process is also very useful when looking at competency-based interviews, which will be discussed in **Chapter 11**.

Critical Incidents Worksheet

List critical incidents from each of your past jobs and what skills and/or achievements were involved.

Job	Critical incident	Skill/achievement

Q88 Describe a typical day in your last job.

This great question offers you the opportunity to **define and establish the way you perceive your job in the most specific of terms** – one specific day's activities and accomplishments. The picture you present should be accurate, but also relevant. Don't give a long, blow-by-blow account, but focus on the activities and tasks which demonstrate your competencies – especially if they are a good match to those required by the job. Give consideration to your **Experience Worksheet** to ensure that you include all the major activities, even if they are not done on a daily basis.

Practise the answer before any meeting, and keep your response within the two-minute range. It is a good practice question because it keeps you aware of recent activities and current issues.

Q89 Describe how your job relates to the overall goals of your department and organization.

All employees, regardless of level, should be aware of how their roles contribute to departmental goals, and how their department relates to the goals of the organization. This relates directly to 'value added' – what value do you add to the organization? This is true for all jobs – not just those in the private sectors.

'Since I was in charge of monitoring budgets, every department relied on my monthly reports to check how close they were to projections. In turn, I was reliant on the various departments for submitting accurate production reports on time. It became a real team effort because there was a profit-sharing incentive in place, so everyone wanted to control expenses and increase production.'

*Q90 Tell me about a major project you've worked on recently.

Ensure that you pick a good example. Here's a good topic for a **Presentation Statement** (see Chapter 6) – a well-rehearsed summary of a recent project that shows you in a good light, has a clear beginning, middle and end, and is something you can communicate to an interviewer in about 3 minutes. (See also Q91.)

Q91 What were the most important projects you completed in your last job?

Again, regardless of job level, use your **Experience Worksheet** and **Critical Incidents Worksheet** prior to your interview to spot anything that you can describe as a 'project', whether it was originally called a project or not.

Most jobs contain projects within them – self-contained work activities that started with a problem and ended, after your personal intervention, with a clear outcome. It might have been something as simple as researching a new supplier, or conducting a feasibility study. If you are at a loss and cannot think of any project at all in your current job, think about your activities outside work. Be careful not to overlook day-to-day projects like moving house, planning your child's education, planning a wedding or holiday, negotiating a mortgage, or providing leadership for an event. There are people all over the country who take responsibility for chairing fund-raising events that are as large and complex as those of the largest organizations. Don't forget to mention one for which you took responsibility.

Q92 How do you normally plan and organize when you are involved in a major or long-term project?

Here use your planning and organizing experience as a reference point to discuss the question in a most effective manner. It does not matter whether the project you are discussing was in or outside work, what is important is to demonstrate quickly and briefly that you know how to plan and organize for a major long-range project. If you have used any specific project management tools or techniques, mention them here, otherwise demonstrate that you are able to take a step-by-step approach, thinking back from the final deadline, and anticipating snags along the way:

'Last year I was responsible for organizing the company sales conference. I start by putting the date in my diary and then working backwards from there to identify all the critical steps, such as booking speakers and confirming travel and accommodation arrangements. Then I look at what needs doing within the next six weeks, and allocate tasks accordingly. The main thing with an event like that is not to let it creep up on you with important things unplanned.'

This is an opportunity for a tag question at the end of your answer (if you feel comfortable in doing so): '*What opportunities will I have to use these skills in this job?*'. This tag-on gets you more details on the scope and nature of the position, and gives you a further opportunity to demonstrate how closely your experience matches the job.

Q93 How many projects can you handle at one time?

You need to balance and hedge. You do not want to portray yourself as a slave who takes an increasing burden of projects and never says no, but you also want to demonstrate a willingness to handle a full workload. A careful answer starts with a review of your own experience to determine what your experience has been.

'*I have had overlap in projects in the past that were completed according to schedule because I had the resources, both personnel and materials, needed to do so.*'

'*I am happy to get involved in a range of projects, but I also know that I have been successful in the past by taking on projects that I know I can complete effectively and on schedule.*'

Q94 What activities did you perform in your last position – and what was the approximate time devoted to these activities?

This question is sometimes phrased, for less senior positions, '*Tell me about a typical working day*'. Consider this a request for a mini job description. When a time balance is requested, rough percentages work effectively. If the job is directly tied to time of day and the work is fairly consistent on a daily basis, then choose a time format.

'I usually reserved the first part of the morning for going through mail, reports, and returning telephone calls. Late mornings I would visit the manufacturing floor, touching base with the various section heads. Afternoons were divided between telephone follow-ups with clients and suppliers, keeping appointments, and weekly meetings with senior management.'

For percentage:

'Days varied considerably, but on a typical day around 30% of my time was spent calling suppliers to ensure that delivery dates continued to be firm. Another 30% was spent researching new product possibilities. About 15% was for correspondence, and 5% for dealing with telephone requests for information. The last 20% was reserved for meetings inside and outside the organization.'

Notice that no percentage is less than 5% and that the total comes to 100%.

Q95 What was/is your workload like on your last/current job?

Now is not the time to complain about how oppressive things were at your last place of employment. If the workload was heavy, say so and provide a few brief details to support your opinion. Relate the details, if possible, to the open position you are interviewing for:

'As in your organization, when we approached the publication date, work escalated and overtime was often required. There was a definite ebb and flow to the workload, with some months, like our double holiday issue, especially frantic, coming at that time of year. The key to my being able to handle the extra work was expecting it to come, because it always did.'

✱Q96 Tell me about a time when you really felt you added value.

Critical incidents are moments where you overcame important problems. One way of looking at them is to think of them as turning points – times when you noticed something going wrong, dealt with a difficult problem, turned something around quickly, made a vital intervention, or took advantage of an opportunity:

'This summer our biggest client started to make noises about being unhappy with the service we were offering. I went straight round and had a meeting with their buyer. The timing was dead right. Later that afternoon he was having a meeting with our main competitor. I put together a 6-point plan for ensuring quality and improved delivery. The buyer thanked me for coming over so promptly and rang me that evening to say we had retained the contract.'

The US department store Nordstrom has a story about a sales assistant who became a legend for customer service. A customer came into the store and returned a set of tyres, and demanded a refund. The assistant gave the refund and took the tyres back. What made the situation a 'critical incident' is that Nordstrom's does not sell tyres. The assistant was adding huge value by offering an unusual level of service. There are organizations who would fire a salesperson for such an action. At Nordstrom's they decided to praise it and make this 'critical incident' a part of their organizational culture because they want their employees to know.

In the UK even managers in supermarkets have been known to take shopping round personally to a problem customer. Going the extra mile is about combining a positive attitude with an imaginative approach to ways of adding value.

Q97 What were your most important work decisions?

This may be asked about your current, previous or a past job. Take a matter-of-fact tone and identify the aspects of your job that gave you the opportunity to make meaningful decisions. The level of the position dictates the weight of the decision. It is perfectly acceptable (in fact, it may be encouraged) to identify the opportunity to make decisions slightly beyond the expected scope of the position, but it is folly to identify as important decisions those which are clearly below your station. A senior buyer may readily mention a '£1m authority level' and an assembly line worker may mention the authority to shut the line down.

Say something about the level of the decision you had to make, the difficulty of making it, and the fact that you made it. The interviewer is in reality probing difficulties you might have making decisions under pressure – so be prepared for a follow-up question along those lines.

Q98 In what ways has your current/last job prepared you to take on greater responsibility?

By reviewing the experiences you encountered during your stay on your last job, you may now well reflect on what your next job should be. The more the situation is similar (if not identical) to the position you are interviewing for, the more the interviewer considers the 'fit':

'When my immediate supervisor was called away for jury service, it was even longer than anticipated – he was tied up for several weeks. During his absence I was responsible for running the division and I enjoyed it immensely. Deadlines and production adhered to schedule, and I was also able to make some recommendations about improved performance when he returned to work, which were well received.'

✶Q99　What is your greatest accomplishment?

Don't go anywhere near a job interview if you haven't prepared some detailed answers about your achievements. If possible, keep your answer focused on work. 'To convince management to proceed with this overseas project – and make it work,' is a grand answer if you have such a situation to draw upon. Spend some time recording your successes – don't make the mistake of believing that you have none. Look for times when you overcame a problem, added value, came up with a good idea, or managed a project to a successful conclusion. A careful review of your past experiences should provide the preparation necessary to field this question in a most effective manner. Be prepared to talk about three elements:

- The problem you had to overcome.
- Your personal contribution.
- The outcome.

　If you can't stick with a work-related situation, identify a situation that is of interest to the interviewer. Practise being a good storyteller. People love brief, interesting stories. Restoration of a house, completing a degree, or planning an interesting expedition would certainly all qualify. The more you are able to confine the discussion to work-related issues, however, the more interviewers see information that they consider strong evidence of a person who gets things done.

Q100　What were your three most significant accomplishments in your last job?

This question is again one you should relish because it is a real opportunity for you to discuss openly what you accomplished. Learn how to communicate accomplishments as short, upbeat stories. For details, you can refer to your **Experience Worksheet**. Consider the question a compliment to you because the person raising the question is most probably a serious, well-trained interviewer. This may appear to be an obvious question, but it is not that frequently asked.

Q101 How do you motivate staff?

Clearly the assumption here is that you are capable of motivating others, but reinforce that with evidence. Go into the interview with several examples of ways you have motivated others. Think about a range of examples, e.g.:

- **Improving or maintaining performance**, for example in sales or customer support roles.
- **Picking people up in difficult situations**, e.g. where others have been laid off.
- **Dealing with underperformers** – where staff have become demotivated.
- **Managing change** – and persuading people to accept it.

Talk about the best situation that you were ever involved with, preferably as an employee but consider any team situation (it may be appropriate here to talk about team sports, or out-of-work activities). Describe the circumstances briefly to show that you have leadership and the ability to take charge if necessary. Talk about a mix of 'push' leadership skills driving people towards goals, and 'pull' leadership skills where communication and intuition help to discover why people are not motivated. Probe, at the end of the interview if necessary, what kind of motivational skills will be required in the new role.

Q102 Do you prefer working with a male or female boss?

This question comes fairly close to unfair discrimination (see **Chapter 13**), because it appears to assume that you will be capable of working more comfortably with managers or colleagues of one sex. Sometimes, for example, it is asked of a male applicant who may be working for a female boss (and is rarely asked the other way – which again indicates poor practice). Here the only answer that you can give is to be honest about the facts of your work history, but give a clear follow-up message that you are entirely flexible and have no hang-ups. The kind of response in answer to any question about male or female bosses or colleagues is simply:

'I can work happily with men or women. What matters is how well somebody does the job.'

'Although all of my bosses have been men, I've often had to work alongside senior female managers from other departments. I'm happy working with a good boss, male or female.'

Q103 How much time on your current/last job is/was spent working alone?

To answer this question well you need to know a little more about the nature of the job. How far does it involve working in teams, with large groups, one-to-one, and how much of your time will be spent working alone? Be prepared to give examples of where you can work effectively in all situations. By showing balance, you eliminate the opportunity for the interviewer to dismiss your application because the job available appears to be unsuitable for the way you normally work.

Be ready for the next obvious question that in all probability follows: **'Which do you prefer?'** State simply that either is an effective environment for you unless you feel strongly that one works and the other doesn't. In that case state it directly and wait for the interviewer's response. If the situation is the opposite of your strong preference, it may be a deal-breaker. And if the balance is completely wrong for you (e.g. you will be working in an isolated one-person office, and you really enjoy being around people and working in a team), then maybe the job isn't for you after all. Remember that a recruiter's job is to find the right person for the job – screening you out for an appropriate reason may be doing you a favour as well.

Q104 How often did you meet up with your boss? Why?

This direct question is an opportunity for interviewers to check out how far you are autonomous, and how far you need close supervision. This should be something you already know a great deal about before the interview commences. It's helpful to compare yourself with others:

'Some people were in and out of the boss's office like yo-yos. I tried to talk to the boss just once a day, first thing, to determine our priorities and identify what was to be accomplished that day. If anything urgent came up, I would try to handle it myself within agreed parameters.'

Q105 How important is it for you to communicate with others at work?

Communication is vital in the workplace. Keeping people informed, motivated and feeling 'in the loop' can make the difference between winning and losing. Regardless of the position, level of position, organization, industry or sector, you need to be convinced of the importance communication plays in every position. Know something about your communication style – do you like to inform people informally, in groups or as you walk around, verbally or in writing? Whatever your normal style, indicate flexibility in approach, depending on the situation, and show how you do it well.

'Communication was very important in my last position because to complete our work successfully, we needed to liaise very closely with the client and learn about problems as quickly as they

occurred. I saw it as my job then to communicate problems and strategies as quickly as possible to everyone on the line – often that meant walking out onto the floor and talking to team leaders, and making sure the message was passed on within 10 minutes.'

Q106 What form of communication do you prefer? Which do you feel is most effective?

Think about the ideal communication environment for the job before you respond. There are times when a quick consultation or a phone call will keep people happy and informed. There are other times when a memo or email is necessary to confirm facts and make sure that others have a file note of deadlines, or points of agreement. Some organizations have a strong culture of written communication; others commit very little to writing. Try to get a feel for the organizational style of this employer before committing yourself to an answer about your preferred method. Any reply that states that you prefer written communication raises concern with most interviewers, because you will give the impression that you are not good with people, and would rather hide behind written correspondence. Interviewers may consider that you prefer protocol and procedure to effective communication and motivation.

'I have always found that direct conversations have been the most effective, with occasional written follow-ups if the situation or the individual makes it necessary.'

Q107 Describe a situation when you had to make a 'seat of the pants' quick decision.

The goal of this question is to determine the ability of the applicant to make a reasonable decision quickly when there is no one to turn to. Your goal is to talk about your ability to respond quickly to changing circumstances. Be careful not to suggest that you assume powers way above your station ('I told the security team to close the whole building...') but try to come across as someone who is not afraid to make a decision if some risk is involved and who recognizes when more risk would be involved by making no decision at all.

'The computers went down in the middle of a senior staff conference. We couldn't get hold of any of the IT managers. What I decided to do was to ask our contractors to come up with an interim solution just to keep things going until the end of the afternoon, and then to provide a full report to my boss for 8.30 am the next day.'

Q108   What was the result of your last appraisal?

Be brief and honest – particularly as this may be reflected in references. Do not elaborate on an issue that you may be particularly sensitive to.

If you have received a formal appraisal within the last 12 months:

'My appraisals were all very positive. In fact, that's the problem. All my appraisals said I had the potential for a more senior role but there just wasn't one available.'

If you didn't have a formal appraisal system:

'We didn't have formal reviews, but on an informal basis a number of people said I was doing a good job and had contributed some good ideas.'

Q109   I see you received only an 'average' rating in your last appraisal. Would you like to comment?

If a negative appraisal is available to the interviewer (e.g. if you are being interviewed for an internal vacancy):

'I was, as you may be aware from my records, given an "average" rating. I don't believe that this really reflected my performance at work. The person responsible for that grading was not my line manager. My own manager was much more positive, taking account of my achievements in ...'

Q110 What things do you find difficult to do? Why?

Identify job elements that are perceived as tedious and of minor importance to the interviewer:

'With everything else going on, I sometimes find it difficult to find the time to keep up with routine emails.'

'Keeping up with paperwork is sometimes difficult if not impossible because new orders are coming in all the time.'

Or talk about an area where you have addressed your own learning needs:

'I used to need help designing new spreadsheets, but I found a really good one-day training programme and I can now produce all the spreadsheets I need.'

Or give your answer a twist and make it a positive 'problem'.

'Because service is such an important hallmark of our approach to internal as well as external customers, I do tend to go out of my way to make sure that people get the help they need.'

Q111 How do you feel if you're asked to do something routine or mundane?

Be careful here. The interviewer may be trying to tell you that the job is a lot less interesting than it looks. If you believe this may be the case, focus the discussion on the way your skills match the position. It's also useful to show a generally positive attitude to routine work:

'I realize that there are times when everyone has to muck in and get things done.'

Q112 How would you rank yourself among your peers?

One of the most difficult things is to speak about ourselves without portraying ourselves on a lower level than we should, or too high (which presents us in a boastful way). This is what makes the question a difficult one. At the same time you must remember that if you don't blow your own trumpet, who will? Try to offer concrete examples of your standing – e.g. when you won an award or were specifically rated against others (e.g. sales turnover, savings, efficiency). You might also think about instances where you were singled out to teach new employees or serve on a special team. If so, share the information.

For the most careful and honest answer, consider the aspects of your ability that you are best at, and then look at those where you could stand improvement. Practise saying both before the meeting. Listen and get others' opinions to determine how 'honest' you need to be without appearing untruthful to yourself.

Q113 Describe the organizational structure in your most recent job.

Review the organization chart from your last/current position, and decide what key pieces of information you are going to communicate verbally.

The best thing is to communicate in terms of job titles, being prepared to say what those titles mean:

'I was responsible to the Assistant Secretary, which in this organization is equivalent to a Departmental Head. I was responsible for a team of 15 staff, including 4 team leaders.'

Reviewing your position in the organization, who you were responsible to and for, should provide insights for you as well as jog your memory. It may be that you never considered that certain reporting relationships were key to job performance.

How does your current or prior organization compare with the organization that you are interviewing with? If you do not know, it is logical for you to ask as long as the interviewer brought up the subject. Point out any positive parallels.

'With the last two foreign banks that I worked at I became very flexible about frequent changes in senior management. I found one key to my success was to remain non-political and show loyalty to the company. As you are part of an international corporation, I imagine the turnover may be quite similar.'

Q114 Have you ever changed the nature of your job? How?

With all the reorganizing taking place in the workplace, in addition to the popularity of self-directed work teams, it would be unusual if your jobs have not undergone a degree of change. What you are looking for here is the opportunity to show that you actively contributed to the way your job was rethought. Any positive answer, either in professional or personal life, shows your creativity and problem-solving ability, and your ability to take control of your own career.

Q115 Tell me about a time when you had to make an unpopular decision.

A review of your **Experience Worksheet** or **Critical Incidents Worksheet** may identify when you had to make an unpopular decision. Now is the time to share it with your interviewer. Do not consider only major situations. Even if as an assistant you needed to bring a matter to the attention of your supervisor risking the wrath of your co-workers, now is the time to mention it. Employers look for loyalty to the organization and supervisors, combined with real experience of tough situations.

'I had to cut a project that my team were really enthusiastic about. The market just wasn't ready for it. I decided the best thing was to take the decision quickly before any further resources were used, and then I was direct about it – emphasizing how much we had all learned from the experience even though we weren't taking it to conclusion. The next task was to remotivate the team by giving them a new challenge.'

Q116 How many levels of management have you had to communicate with? On what issues and levels did you deal with management?

The interviewer is trying to determine the range of your contacts in your last position. In an effort to give substance to your answer, and also as a reality check, provide the functional and corporate title (never the name) and briefly describe the purpose and extent of the contact:

'In addition to the ongoing contact with the Marketing Director, and the District Sales Manager, I had to deal with the relocation officer for a major move our department was going through and see the Financial Director monthly to discuss budget variances.'

Q117 What problems have you identified that had previously been overlooked?

Here is a chance to shine by being prepared. The interviewer is trying to determine your ability to see beyond the confines of the day-to-day activities of the position to significantly improve the position's output and effectiveness. A major reason for bringing someone in to fill a position from the outside is to get a fresh look at the situation and bring new ideas. You want the interviewer to think 'can do' and 'will do', and raise the hope that you have new solutions in your repertoire.

Q118 On what basis were you able to determine if you were doing a good job?

This should be a cakewalk of a question, but unfortunately it frequently is not. All employees, regardless of job position, location, industry or sector, should be able to assess their own performance level periodically. If workers do not do this, they are at the mercy of the person who evaluates them in an appraisal. By periodically determining the level of your own performance, you become a consistent benchmark and evaluator of your own performance.

'I think my results spoke for themselves ... Within 12 months we became the UK's main provider of external training courses in this field.'

Q119 What do you think is the most difficult aspect of being a manager/executive?

'Giving bad news' is as succinct and to the point as one can get. This answer provides a brief valid answer that begs the serious interviewer to ask you for more. A superficial interviewer does not pursue with additional questions to flesh out your thought-provoking response and to determine whether there is substance and a demonstration of in-depth experience behind the answer. This response addresses how a manager reacts to difficult situations.

A second response demonstrates that the manager is ready to take control and provide leadership from the start. *'Getting the group of people that you have inherited to respond quickly and effectively to your authority.'*

Motivating people and finding (as well as building) the team are additional areas to explore in finding an effective approach to this question. Both certainly demonstrate to the interviewer the depth of your experience and your ability to be trusted with the responsibility for managing others.

Q120 What do you think makes this position different from your last one?

Look for a positive trait that distinguishes the two roles. If that positive trait demonstrates that you will be a strong employee, then you are successfully answering the question.

'The team is more committed.'

'The management appears more supportive.'

'The challenges are greater.'

Q121 What unfinished business have you left behind that you wish you had concluded?

Best here not to talk about anything that you should, in all honesty, have completed, but to express an interest in long-term ideas, preferably drawing upon skills and enthusiasm that will transfer:

'I would really have liked to see how we could have started to develop e-business opportunities – in fact, that's one of the things that appeals to me most about this job…'

Another approach is to target specific changes in the process: *'The introduction of new technology, a turnaround time of less than 20 minutes, lower turnover.'* These are all perfectly acceptable alternatives because they allow the interviewer to think again 'can do – will do'.

Q122 What kind of decisions are most difficult for you?

Identify those that involve either a human relations issue or a lower or subordinate level. Concentrate on those dealing with tough choices:

'Do I give the person another chance who has just broken the machinery for the third time?'

'Do I vote to close the plant because for the last three quarters productivity has been falling and one of four plants must be closed?'

Q123 What makes you think you could handle a position that requires such a range of skills and experience?

This question is a positive alternative to the query 'You don't seem to have all the experience I want, why should I appoint you?'. Even when presented with the question in this way, reply alertly. Talk separately about skills and experience:

'*It's my understanding that this position requires the following skills… Is that correct?*' List them briefly and stop. If you do this in a gentle way, you get the interviewer's buy-in.

Proceed carefully in case interviewers are distracted or feel that you are now quizzing them. The second reason to be extremely careful is so that, when listing the talents and skills, you select and emphasize those that play to your strengths.

'I feel that my current position has many demands for skills, and I have been able to meet the demands thus far with great success. My special ability to be a quick learner and intuitive about other people's ability has enabled me to react to situations as needed.'

If the interviewer cites a skill that you apparently do not have and that is felt to be essential to the position, unless it is an obvious one, ask what aspect of the job requires it. You may cause the interviewer to rethink the job, reconsider the job requirements, or open the door to alternative skills or experience that you do have.

'It is true that I do not have hands-on experience with WordPerfect but Word for Windows is so similar I feel confident that it will not take any time to be proficient. In fact, current upgrades make the two programs even more compatible.'

Q124 What do you look for when *you* are recruiting?

If you feel you have no experience of recruiting, it's probably best to say so at this point. Were you involved in any way in the recruitment process? Remember times when you were not an employee (for example, as a volunteer in a not-for-profit organization or in a situation where you had to serve as a home care provider). In this situation, you may have had the opportunity to hire one or more individuals but you may not recall the situation because it occurred outside the workplace.

You will be asked this if your job involves recruitment and selection, but you may also be asked it as a general interview question. In a way, what it's really doing is saying: 'What do you think we're looking for?'. You can safely talk about the mainstream characteristics found in strong applicants, e.g. sound work ethic, loyalty, knowledge, dedication, and a 'can-do' attitude, but your answer will be even stronger if it adds to the job description:

'It's clear that you're looking for a good organizer, and somebody who is capable of researching things in detail. I think if I was recruiting for this post I'd also be interested in someone who had an interest in taking advantage of new technology...'

There may be a hidden agenda going on work: defining your own qualities. Do you demonstrate the characteristics that you have defined as vital? It's worth remembering that, on the simplest level, a recruiter has three basic ingredients for a successful selection decision:

1. 'CAN DO'
   The candidate has the **ability** to do the job, and the right competences (see **Chapter 11**).
2. 'WILL DO'
   The candidate has done the job in the past, or something similar. Alternatively, the candidate demonstrates potential to grow into the role.
3. 'FIT'
   The candidate has skills and qualities which are an excellent match to the job, team, and organization.

Show You Are a 'Can Do' Candidate

■ 'There is no substitute for experience.' **Look at your past work history** to evaluate your types of experience.

■ If you do not have the kind of experience that is desired, do not 'invent' it. Is there a comparable job skill or experience that can be offered?

■ Should you find yourself lacking experience for which there is no substitute, **start getting training now**. Attend workshops and seminars.

■ **Become known in your field**. Join and take an active role in professional organizations. Attend conferences and become acquainted with as many of your peers as possible.

■ **Share your knowledge** by teaching, doing workshops and seminars.

Competency-based Interviews

QUESTIONS YOU WILL FACE

Employers want to know about skills. The problem is that in most interviews a recruiter has to make an informed guess about the standard of the skill you have used, and how well you may be able to engage this skill in the future. Applicants can say that they can operate a piece of equipment, but the employer never knows until they are hired if they can really do it – unless a work sample test is provided during the selection process. A well-trained interviewer will however seek solid evidence from you about your skills, possibly focusing on competencies.

What is a 'competency'?

A **competency** is, in its simplest form, a set of 'performance behaviours'. One of the proponents of this idea was Richard Boyatzis who defined a competency as 'an underlying characteristic of an individual which is causally related to effective or superior performance'. A competency is therefore not just a skill, but is a combination of know-how, skills, attitude and demonstrated behaviours – all directed towards outcomes which actively assist an employer. A competency is not just about what you do, but how you do it.

A simple example is answering the telephone. A competent operator will be able to answer a phone within a prescribed number of rings and deal efficiently with a customer. An above-average performer will display a fully-rounded set of competencies by also making the customer feel informed and valued. In this context, the competency might be defined as 'Giving excellent customer service in telephone contacts'.

This description is typical of a competency. Others for someone in a customer service role might be:

- The ability to handle multiple tasks under time pressure.
- The ability to prioritize workloads.
- A flexible, open style – coping with the unexpected on a daily basis.

Behavioural questions are at the heart of competency-based interviews. This model focuses far less on 'biographical' information about you (e.g. your schooling, your personality, and your past and present motivation) and puts far more emphasis on what you have done in the past, and how you did it.

Biographical Interviews Focus on:	Competency-based Interviews Focus on:
Education	Skills
Qualifications	Achievements
Training	Attitudes
Work History	Values
Personal history	Knowledge put into practice
Family background	Observable behaviours
Availability	
Motivation	

The behavioural approach contends that **past performance is the best predictor of future performance** ('can do' – 'will do again'). In behavioural questioning, the interviewer asks applicants to supply evidence of past events which demonstrate all the elements that go into a competency: the skills you possess, the attitudes you demonstrate, the knowledge and values you bring to the job.

Look at the clues available to you about job content, and complete the **Competency Worksheet** below. Work out (either from the Job Description or from your own good judgement) which competencies are going to be most important in this role. Rank these competencies on a scale of 1 to 5. In the right hand column, write down a matching experience. This chart will help you to consider how your strengths and weaknesses may affect your 'fit' to the position. When considering the behaviours required in the open position, look for alternatives. For example, you may have not worked as a marketing assistant, but even as a PA you may have had some input in the past into the way brand values are communicated to customers.

Competency Worksheet

Organization:

Position:

Rank competencies as essential (1) or desirable (2)

Competencies required in position	Ranking	Examples when I have used these competencies

✱Q125 You are aware that we are looking for candidates who have demonstrated the ability to _____. How does this match your experience?

Prepare for questions in this area by giving careful considera-tion to all the competencies that you have identified as being essential to the job. You can spot these in a number of ways:

1. Where specific **competencies** are listed and defined by the organization. You may have completed a written statement which asks you to give detailed information about times when you have used a series of competencies.
2. Where the job description and/or advertisement talk about a mix of skills, knowledge and attitudes.
3. Where the job is defined in terms of activities, targets or outcomes – work back from those to establish what kind of behaviours will be needed to achieve them.

Even when it comes to basic competencies, make sure you have good examples and detail. If you are talking about filing as a competency, identify a time when you dealt with some-thing difficult or unusual.

Q126 Where *exactly* have you used this competency?

This kind of probing question may be used specifically in relation to a competency, or may be asked much more gener-ally about skills. The trick here is to prepare your evidence in advance, and decide how you are going to communicate it. Learn a series of mini-narratives to communicate

■ The **problem or situation** you had to deal with.
■ What **you, personally did** in response – focusing on your competencies.
■ The **outcome or result** you achieved.

Q127 Tell me about a responsibility in your current/last job that you really enjoyed.

Be careful not to throw this gift question away. Even though it should be easy, carefully determine your answer in advance. This is sometimes a 'one-two' question that is immediately followed by a request for you to identify the responsibility you really liked least.

In an ideal situation, concentrate on the most important aspects of your position – the most creative, the most project-oriented, the most essential to the organization – or the aspects that provided you with the most visibility. A very senior member of the management of one of the world's major banks used to always say, '*An organization can never have enough good people. If you meet one as a job applicant and you don't have a job to offer, hire him or her, make the hire anyway, and find something for the person to do.*' Too frequently, however, interviewers are more interested in screening out rather than screening in *and this question could be the decision-maker.* If you are being considered for a position well below your last one, you may be giving the interviewer an opportunity to dismiss you.

Talk with enthusiasm and energy about areas of responsibility – and make sure that your evidence includes reference to achievements.

Q128 Give an example where you had to be _____ on the job.

This question gives interviewers the opportunity to determine how you exhibit a certain trait or characteristic that they feel is essential to the position. The missing word might be neutral ('assertive') or provocative ('ruthless'). You should be well prepared for this question having reviewed the **Competency Worksheet.** Given the list you prepared, what additional characteristics do you feel are essential to the job or detrimental to your application?

Depending on the trait and the interviewer's agenda, *this question can either screen in or screen out candidates*. Traits can be viewed either as a positive or as a negative. Take, for example, the adjectives 'creative' and 'aggressive'. Creativity in an advertising manager is a laudable trait; in an accountant, creative bookkeeping entries could cause problems. Aggressiveness in sales managers who push into new markets could be exactly what a start-up company needs, but aggressiveness is not what a child care agency requires. All positions should be viewed as offering opportunities to exhibit most personal traits, and can be a greater or lesser part of the position's responsibility. For the 'creative' accountant, a response could be:

'I find that all the different types of clients and their individual business needs require a creative mind to solve their problems. No two clients are alike, and I feel that my secret to my success is making them feel that they get individual service created for their individual needs.'

Q129 Describe a complex problem that you had to deal with.

To prepare an answer to this question, refer back to your **Experience Worksheet** and **Critical Incidents Worksheet** (**Chapter 10**). When reviewing accomplishments, select one of the most meaningful and consider it from a level of complexity. Pick a situation that shows you to be an effective organizational player. For the word 'problem' substitute 'project' if it helps to clarify appropriate situations.

'I've handled a number of complex problems just in the last couple of months. One example would be the IT support behind setting up a centralized accounting function. My first task was to write the project planning document, and to do this I had to interview all the departmental heads to find out exactly what

they needed and when. Next I had to put together a specification so that we could put the technical side out to tender...'

Be aware of **time lines**. *The longer the time frame between the start of a project and its completion, the greater the responsibility.* Lower-level personnel may deal with daily pressures and deadlines; higher management looks to longer-range projects and deadlines. Position your response accordingly.

Q130 When have you coached someone to become more effective?

It's common to be asked questions about developing, coaching and mentoring other members of staff. Don't get into too much detail (it may be confidential anyway), but briefly describe the situation or problem you were trying to resolve, what style of intervention you used, and what results were achieved. This will demonstrate that you are able to keep two things in focus: organizational objectives, and the needs of the individual you have helped.

Q131 Have you ever had difficulty getting along with others?

If your answer presents you in a positive light, then give it as a strong answer.

'As a matter of fact, yes. When I was a student I found temporary work with a distribution company. I had problems from the start because I wanted to show how productive I could be. Every day, even though I was new, I was setting productivity records. The union steward and then a few of my fellow workers tried to dissuade me by letting me know in very direct language that I was disruptive and my work habits needed to change or I would encounter difficulty in my work relationships. Even my supervisor

felt the need to tell me to slow down. I felt it was diplomatic to find work somewhere else.'

If you do not have a strong answer like this, just state that you have always found a common ground to deal with others to accomplish the job at hand.

Q132 Describe a situation where you needed to get an understanding of another's viewpoint before you could get your job done. What problems did you encounter and how did you handle them?

Consider a situation where you and a colleague had a major difference of opinion regarding an action plan or a definition of a problem that you were both expected to solve. This kind of scenario frequently serves to address this question. What frequently exacerbates the problem is a personality conflict, and the working relationship may be marred by issues unrelated to work. Whatever you do, *never identify a scenario that may lead the interviewer to think that you may be the problem*, because the questions raised about where the real problem lies are greater and more memorable than the issues the story is intended to resolve.

Q133 How did you get along with your last team?

Team working is a highly regarded competency, so avoid negatives. If you have anything negative to say, it can only be done in the context of, '*I was much more interested in getting the job done than they were.*' Otherwise, you were very effective in your dealings with them, and in fact there was real cohesion in the group. (Provide one or two examples of how the group drew together in a 'crisis' situation.)

Q134 Tell me about a difficult situation when you pulled the team together.

Identify a situation that led to a positive outcome and be careful during the answering of the question to mix 'we' and 'I' to demonstrate that you were an active participant of the group but also made a distinctive contribution.

'When the most highly regarded member of our five-person team resigned, I had to break the news not only that was she leaving but that she would not be replaced. I then told the team that we would meet in two days to map out a strategy to determine how we were going to accomplish the same results with only four people. For the next two days (right up to the meeting), I visited each person (including the departing employee) to assess their morale and their level of concern. I mentioned to each of them that the business was going through a downturn and we really needed each person's participation to help the organization get through this difficult time. I must have got through – when we had our next team meeting they said they would give me their total support, and offered some practical strategies for what we could do next.'

Q135 Describe a situation when the team fell apart. What was your role in the outcome?

Do not be concerned here about the 'failure' aspect of the question. The interviewer wants to know how you deal with a team that is under-performing. Your answer will show two key aspects: *first, that you recognize problems when they occur and, second, that you are able do something about them.*

'One of our team responsibilities was finding a way to integrate two departments. The problem was that the team was composed of members of staff from both companies, and no-one wanted to give an inch. We resolved this by using an entirely theoretical model, using "red" and "green" to describe the different functions,

and deliberately seeking solutions that were a win/win for each side of the equation.'

Q136 **When you begin to work with new people, how do you get to understand them? Are you successful in predicting/interpreting their behaviour? Give examples.**

Listening is the key to getting to understand another person. When you start with a new work team, they have an advantage over you: they need to understand just one person – you. You, on the other hand, must get to understand each and every one of them. Additionally, even with excellent listening skills, it is still difficult to predict a person's behaviour each and every time. To answer this question in a strong, confident manner, it is important to say at the start that you have had a great deal of success predicting and interpreting other people's behaviour, but also mention that it does not always work. Then proceed with a brief example or two.

'An MBA we had hired needed to be told that one of her responsibilities would include increased time on the switchboard. This was not a surprise because during the recruiting and selection process we had emphasized in our discussions the "hands-on" culture of our organization and she had confirmed throughout that she realized that this is something she may be called on to do once she joined us. I realized that the most important thing was not just to assume that she would take on these duties, but to reinforce the idea that she was doing what other members of the team do. Introduced this way, the request was accepted.'

Q137 **Describe a situation where you failed to reach a goal.**

Interviewers try to determine how you deal with adversity and see if you have a need to win every time. Identify a situation where you had to adjust your sights and, if possible, go back to succeed at a later date. Succeeding, however, is not as important as your demonstration of an ability to deal with tough times as well as good.

University may be one example, for instance, if you had to delay higher education because of personal circumstances. Do not let bitterness come through.

In work contexts, it's useful to refer to failures that were outside your control but helped to bring a team together or provided a useful learning experience.

'I had submitted a training proposal to a recruitment company – at their request. Many meetings were held, with senior management requesting revisions in the programme, which I accommodated. The meetings never resulted in a signed contract, however, because the HR manager left in the middle of negotiations to work for a competitor. However it gave us a real insight into the needs of the recruitment industry, and we gained three new clients on the back of a new sales training programme.'

Q138 Describe circumstances where you had to work under pressure.

This should be an easy one for everyone, but do not take it for granted. Review your worksheets and consider the best, most recent story that the interviewer is most likely to relate to. If pressure is a daily event, mention that fact and talk about routine and non-routine pressure, and how you respond in a crisis.

This kind of question is often directed at those returning to the workplace. Come armed with examples to reassure the interviewer that you haven't lost touch with what it's like to deal with workplace pressure:

'I've been concerned not to lose my "edge", so I enjoyed the opportunity to organize a number of big fund-raising events for our

local hospice. Believe me, organizing sponsorship, guest speakers, and selling 300 places is no picnic – especially when you only have 12 weeks from start to finish.'

Q139 We have a continuing problem with _____. How would you handle that?

Demonstrate your specific work experience and mirror the situation described – but you might begin by asking for a little more detail. No consultant or manager jumps in with a solution without understanding exactly what is going on. Once you have established the key facts, put forward a brief, realistic but interesting answer. If you have a 'been there, done that' experience, now is the time to highlight it.

A threefold strategy works well with this kind of question:

1. Clarify what the problem is. How big? How critical?
2. Find out what strategies have been tried (and what solutions the employer sees as possible, unless the interviewer is really not giving much away).
3. Offer solutions which match your experience and achievements, e.g. *'In the past what I've found helpful is to conduct a quick survey of all the tools and strategies being used across departments and share best practice – better than reinventing the wheel.'*

Q140 What would you do if you had to make a decision that wasn't covered by the rule book?

This is a double-edged question. It could be trying to find out whether you can 'think outside the box', but it can also be used to check how far you conform within corporate guidelines. Consider what environment you prefer to work in: one with few rules and the excitement of the unknown – or within a strict environment of rules and procedures?

Q141 How do you interact with different management levels?

You need to show that you are accustomed to interacting with different management levels. Try to show a balance of confidence and tact. Indicate with a brief answer the variety of unit heads that you have had to deal with and the issues you had to deal with.

'I mentioned an idea in passing to the MD, and he asked me to make an appointment to see him the next day to explain it in detail. I knew he doesn't like excessive detail, so I made sure I had thought through the advantages and disadvantages of my proposal, and I set them out clearly in a brief summary document. I got him to say yes in five minutes, and I got to be in charge of the project.'

Management Competencies

This chapter includes a range of questions about management competencies and experience. The reason? You are far more likely to come across a discussion of competencies if you are going for a management role. Even if you are not in a management role at the moment, don't forget that employers will often be screening candidates for management potential.

There are many different ways of describing management competencies, but you will find that the six listed at the bottom of the **Management Competencies** table below are high up in the lists produced by current management theory.

Management Competencies	
Planning	Delegating
Organizing	Directing (leading)
Controlling	Prioritizing
Informing	Motivating
Objective setting	Trouble-shooting

Management and Leadership

One classic distinction is that management is about doing things right, and leadership is about doing the right thing. In other words, management is focused on getting things done, while leadership is about deciding *what* needs to be done, and taking others with you on the way.

'Leadership' is also used as a term to describes a set of competencies for effective managers. Interviewers may use the terms 'manager' and 'leader' interchangeably – but it helps if you are aware of the competencies that are about management (e.g. organizing resources and people, trouble-shooting, setting objectives) and leadership (e.g. seeing the big picture, having a sense of vision, empowering and inspiring). So clarify which you are talking about if you feel you and the interviewer are not both discussing the same attributes. The questions in **Are You a Manager or A Leader?** below may prove helpful.

Are You a Manager or a Leader?

Compare column A to column B. In each row tick the statement that most closely matches the way you generally work.

A	or	B
Do you work within boundaries?		Do you expand boundaries?
Do you control resources?		Do you influence others?
Are you making plans to reach goals?		Are you working to create a future?
Are you responsible for when and how work is done?		Do you commit to get the work done at any cost?

Do you follow rules and systems?	Do you rewrite the rules when you face new situations?
Do past events and precedents dictate present actions?	Does your vision for the future dictate present actions?
Do you make decisions only after all relevant information is available?	Do you decide when you feel you have *enough* information?
Do you encourage others?	Do you inspire others?
Do you worry about making the right decision?	Do you feel that the important thing is to make a decision and stick to it?
Do you measure performance against plans?	Do you measure accomplishments against your vision of the future?
Total:	Total:

Scoring: Column A scores are broadly about management qualities, while ticks in column B indicate leadership characteristics.

Regardless of your level professionally, consider a situation where you had the opportunity to get things done through others (that's what management is all about) and recall what made you effective or ineffective. Did you communicate effectively? Did you encourage teamwork? Emphasize quality and/or results? Did you get your hands dirty?

Q142 How do you manage people?

You should have already considered this question as part of a self-assessment in preparation for any job search effort. *There are two major approaches: one emphasizes tasks and the other stresses relationships.* They are not necessarily mutually exclusive, nor should they ever be, according to the management experts. In the traditional sense, managers were portrayed in a maintenance mode and reactive in a bureaucratic setting; leaders, on the other hand, were proactive, looked for problems and issues before they occurred, and were results-driven and entrepreneurial in thinking.

Q143 Give an example of a time when you have displayed leadership qualities.

Leadership, in the eyes of recruiters, translates into a number of key areas as demonstrated by the **Are You a Manager or a Leader?** checklist. Your pre-prepared evidence should communicate characteristics which are relevant to the position on offer, which may include:

- Decision-making (particularly under tough conditions).
- Setting visionary goals.
- Redefining what the organization does.
- Exploring new territory.
- Launching new products or ideas.
- Inspiring staff to improve their performance.
- Keeping colleagues committed and focused.

Q144 What contribution did you make to the management team?

Often candidates use the word 'we' rather than 'I' to give credit for the accomplishments of others in the team. That's fine, but it's vital that you are able to say how you contributed to any team you were part of. Were you the ideas person, the co-ordinator, the project driver? Or perhaps you were the person who stopped the other members of the team strangling each other?

Positive Team Contributions

■ Accepting responsibility for problems.
■ Encouraging other team members.
■ Keeping other team members 'in the loop'.
■ Supporting decisions (even you're when not happy about them).
■ Sharing success and not allocating blame.
■ Being optimistic in tough situations.

Q145   Tell me about a time when you took a tough decision as a manager.

Prepare carefully to present evidence of times you have trained, supervised, managed or led others, particularly under difficult circumstances. You might want to focus your examples on key management functions, such as controlling, directing and organizing:

'Relocation expenses were out of control when I took responsibility for the function. I reviewed the records [control], *and worked with experienced staff to determine where we were spending money carelessly. My team made a series of recommendations and drafted a new set of guidelines* [direct]. *We then set up a work-flow system to maximize the effectiveness of the new procedures* [organize].'

Do not panic if you have never managed in a paid capacity; it's likely that you have done so either personally with your family or as part of voluntary or community activities. Prepare before the meeting to identify situations that you were personally involved in that demanded management expertise. If you recently left full-time education, consider any organizations you helped to run or any activities (a dance, raffle, concert) that you actively worked to promote.

Determine which of those duties that you performed required help from others, and provide evidence of ways you persuaded others to help you achieve a result. This evidence can be of high value because, in many ways, managing volunteers is more demanding than managing paid staff.

Q146   How persistent are you?

This is a fine-line question because what is perceived to be persistent to one person may be regarded as stubborn, inflexible or argumentative by someone else. What is persistence? Let's define it here as *the ability and desire of a person to stick with an issue until its resolution (which may include acceptance or rejection)*. If rejection is the decision, additional persistence may or may not be a positive characteristic, and the judgement of the person involved becomes increasingly a major issue. It's useful to know when to let go of pet projects or new ideas.

   Is persistence a positive or negative characteristic? Regardless of the intent of the interviewer, start with your positive spin on the characteristic and pay particularly close attention to the interviewer to determine his or her opinion and feelings about persistence. You may start by saying:

'I feel that to be effective in an organization a certain amount of persistence is required.'

   Then proceed to say:

'In answer to your question I am a persistent person. Let me give you a situation that demonstrates my use of persistence to complete a project.'

   Then you move on to the second part of the question and tell about what action you performed that demonstrates your persistence in a favourable light. Your story may well bring out other competencies at the same time such as problem-solving, improvising under pressure, and assertiveness.

One HR professional recalls the story told by a Gulf War veteran who decided to defend a friend of his who had been falsely accused of being absent without leave while on guard duty. The ex-soldier demonstrated how with no legal training he identified the authorities he needed to deal with, conducted research, and, because of his doggedness, was able to get the charges swiftly dismissed. This is a good example that **not only brings out the complexity of the problem succinctly but incorporates a personal characteristic – in this case, persistence.**

Q147 How far do you see yourself rising in our organization?

Be realistic. If you can be vague and you want to take that tack, certainly do so: '*I would like to rise as high as my skills and opportunities here permit.*' If it works and there is no follow-up question, you are off the hook and chances are the interviewer is either distracted or very inexperienced and/or untrained. Chances are that you need to provide a little more detail.

Consider your field of expertise as one avenue, and talk about responsibilities rather than job titles:

'*I would like to eventually be responsible for the marketing function.*'

'*I'd like to be able to run my own client list.*'

Top tips for discussing your competencies

■ *Be objective*; know yourself.
■ Answer the questions directly; do not ramble.
■ Use the **appropriate vocabulary** level; do not overuse jargon.
■ Think of evidence in terms of situation, contribution and result.

- **Listen** as much as you talk. Pick up clues about how the interviewer sees the competency being discussed.
- Don't rush in with glib solutions; listen and share ideas.
- Think about competencies, skills and behaviours. Remember that a competency is about *how* you exercised a set of skills.
- Talk about behaviours and outcomes that demonstrate your **attitude** and **values**.
- **Present evidence** to support your claims.
- Talk about your team involvement, but make sure you talk about your personal contribution.
- Think of evidence of **management** and **leadership**.

Difficult Questions

CAN YOU TAKE THE HEAT?

A long-standing interviewer tradition once favoured by traditional employers was to submit candidates to a stressful interview to determine if they are 'tough enough' to handle a gruelling job. Research results repeatedly demonstrate that stress interviews are not valid predictors of job performance: all they predict is that people are good at handling stressful interviews. Stress-inducing interviews are ineffective because they don't encourage candidates to disclose useful information. However, many interviewers hang on to some aspects of the stressful interviewing style – usually demonstrated through difficult, oddball or so-called 'killer' questions.

Stress – the Ever Present Factor in Interviews

Whether the employer consciously decides to inject it or not, there will always be a degree of stress in the interview process. For the interviewer it's a routine conversation. For the job candidate an interview is a potentially life-changing event. Secondly, it's personal – ultimately it's about *you* and what you have to offer.

There's no point beating yourself up because you find interviews stressful. Most people do. It's better to work out how stress inhibits you or reduces your performance, and prepare in advance to compensate. If you are poor at coming up with good examples in the interview room, prepare them in detail in advance. If you know that you are uncomfortable talking about a particular topic (e.g. why you left university without completing your degree), prepare a short, clear and positive **Presentation Statement** in advance (see **Chapter 6**).

There are many things that contribute to stress on the day. Being asked to wait because interviews are delayed will raise tension, and being late because your journey was delayed will certainly raise your blood pressure. Some people find unexpected events stressful – e.g. being asked to take some kind of test without warning, or discovering that the 'friendly chat' is actually a panel interview. However, the better your preparation, the easier it is to cope with unanticipated events.

The furniture may also contribute to stress. A subsidiary of a major Japanese bank had futons available for job applicants in its Human Resource reception area. There were no choices. It was futons or stand. They were easy enough to sit on and comfortable too. The problem with the futons, though, was that they were impossible to get up from without some very awkward moments for both male and female candidates.

The receptionist and other staff coming into contact with job candidates may provide additional stress moments. There's nothing worse than arriving at reception and being told that no-one is expecting you – but it happens. Being greeted by an interviewer who thinks you are somebody else has a similar effect. Before the interview even starts, candidates have to expend valuable energy and confidence to get to where they were supposed to be in the first place, and they are easily thrown by off-putting events. That is why a professional recruitment process takes candidate stress seriously, for example by sending out clear instructions about where, when and how you will be interviewed, and making sure you are put at your ease when you arrive.

Stress Makers and Breakers

Stress Makers	Stress Breakers
■ The interview itself	■ Prepare; know your material
■ Probing questions	■ Prepare your evidence so that it is capable of being mined for detail
■ Personality questions	■ Don't apologize or boast. Be aware of your strengths and weaknesses
■ Skill questions	■ Don't over-claim. Be prepared to give a clear idea of how well you exercise a skill
■ Vague questions	■ Politely ask the interviewer to define the terms of the question
■ Awkward, off-the-wall or fantasy questions	■ Keep focused on the job
■ Unlawful questions	■ Move on quickly without getting into a battle
■ Silence during the interview; internal pressure to keep on talking	■ Accept silence; avoid being intimidated to speak more. Don't over-disclose.
■ Negative reactions from the interviewer	■ Prepare presentation statements to cover negative areas ■ Don't over-supply information
■ Offer to smoke or have a beverage	■ Limit chances for further anxiety and say 'no thanks'
■ Mealtime interview	■ Recognize that you are not there to eat; you are there to get a job. Order simple dishes you can eat without getting into difficulties
■ Inexperienced, antagonistic, unprepared or bored interviewer	■ Be adaptable. Offer clear, concise answers. Read body language to see if you are getting your points across

However, there are still many organizations out there who organize things less than perfectly, and sadly many interviewers who believe that stress-inducing circumstances or questions are useful ways of testing how you operate under pressure. So, in general, be prepared for things moving in an unpredictable fashion. How do you prepare for the unexpected? Largely by doing enough homework and preparation in advance so that you can cope with a variety of questions and *keep your answers focused on the needs of the organization.*

A lot of questions in this book (possibly all of them) may increase the stress level of the candidate. In this chapter we consider the questions that are the most difficult, stressful or intimidating. The table **Stress Makers and Breakers** (page 195) explores a range of initial strategies.

Q148   **What kind of person are you?**

It's tricky to answer a vague question like this. Is the question about your working style, your preferences, your interpersonal skills, or what you are like outside work? Should your answer be a single sentence or a full summary? Best to seek clarification quickly:

'What aspects would you like me to talk about?'

See also **Question 30** for more ideas on a similar question.

Q149   **What do you want to get out of today's meeting?**

It's tempting to answer 'a job offer', and that might be an appropriate response. However, some first interviews are really explorations on both sides, so it's probably a good idea to talk in more general terms about your objectives for any meeting. You also need a clear idea of the interviewer's role in the selection process – are you talking to someone who is involved in initial screening or will make the final selection decision? Is the interviewer someone you may be working with in the future?

Be clear about your aim. Is there a job under discussion, or is the company simply talking to you because you appear to be interesting? If there is no defined job, your initial response to this question will inevitably be open:

'I understand that you don't have a defined vacancy at the moment, but I believe that you're interested in moving into _____. At this stage I think it's sensible for us to talk about where you're going at the moment as a company.'

Use a salesperson's approach: don't try to make a pitch too early. Find out what the organization's needs are (seek problems and opportunities) and, ideally, ask your interviewer for his or her proposed solution. Then, and only then, talk about the way you match the organization; otherwise you sound as if you are making a sales pitch before understanding what the company is looking for. On the other hand, don't say that you are only looking for information. If interviewers have a job available, they may not share that fact with you until they know what you have to offer.

Note: Information interviews are frequently encouraged by outplacement and other career counsellors, but they are problematic because they can have a confused agenda. See John Lees' *How To Get A Job You'll Love* for a discussion of the **REVEAL** method of informational interviews, designed specifically for career changers in the UK and Europe. An informational interview is only there to provide you with details about job roles, career routes, and particular industries or fields. It is **not** a covert job interview. If there is any possibility that an interviewer is trying to make a selection decision, you should consider the meeting as a job interview and prepare accordingly.

If you have honestly spoken to the person you are meeting

with about the true purpose of the meeting, you might say, for example, '*I was hoping that I would be able to convince you that I'm the right person for the job.*'

*Q150 What do you know about our organization?

If you are unprepared for this one, you should not be sitting in this meeting in the first place. Even for courtesy interviews, be prepared by finding out whatever you can about the organization with whom you will be meeting. Consider the question from a selfish point of view:

- Why is this organization for you?
- What makes this organization exceptional?
- What value can you offer to this organization?

You owe it to yourself to learn as much as you can about any organization that you intend to visit. What you choose to share, however, really takes fine judgement on your part. If you uncover something adverse, you do not want to mention it here. If meeting with a television company, now is not the time, for example, to speak about the appalling lack of quality in children's programming.

Provide a concise overview of your findings that shows you are aware of what the organization does and the size of its operations. '*XYZ is a consultancy focused on the retail sector. I understand the business went through a management buy-out last year I read that you have four offices and plan to open two more in the next year.*' If you show some knowledge about the organization, especially if the information is not that easy to obtain, you make a good impression. Be careful not to overwhelm the interviewer with detail – you only have to show that you are a reasonable enquirer, not an expert. And beware above all else the '*I could of course do it a lot better*' tone of voice.

Q151 What do you know about the position for which you are applying?

This is a good opportunity to clear the air. If you have a lot of information about the position, speak confidently and briefly. If you have little or no information, say so. But don't confess to total ignorance if you could have found out plenty about the job from the company's website. *Rule of thumb: a little information is a better response than none.* If you have no information about the position, the burden is on you to have a reason for applying for a position about which you know nothing – not an impossible situation, but usually somewhat odd. This is a question you should ask yourself regularly as you go through the selection process, and salient facts should be marked on your **Organization Fact Sheet** (see **Chapter 2**).

Is the Position for You?

■ Make sure it is a position that you really want to pursue.
■ Regularly update your information concerning the position.

Don't forget that the purpose of the interview is to share information; don't be afraid to get additional information about the position if you need to.

Q152 What is your overall impression of this organization?

Based on your professional knowledge and instincts, you should be prepared for this question because you should have asked it of yourself. If subtitles were provided for this question, they would be, '*Why do you want this job?*' and '*Why do you want to work here?*'. Provide the interviewer with a short, focused answer. This is an opportunity to show the depth of your knowledge and the reach of your contacts by *sharing briefly what you have learned about the organization from your research and from the interview process itself.*

Q153 What do you identify as our biggest opportunity? What do you feel is our major advantage over our competition?

Here is an opportunity to show not only that you did your homework in preparing for this meeting but that you have great professional bearing and an in-depth knowledge of the industry and its other key players. Again, do not overwhelm. Do not show up interviewers by discussing a topic in more detail than they are equipped to handle. Also, as far as problems are concerned, try to avoid controversy. Don't bring up matters regarding litigation, bad publicity, or disgruntled past members of staff you may have met. Instead, select a product-related problem like the rising cost of newsprint if you happen to be meeting with a print media organization. Talk in positive terms about what you have appreciated about the organization's brand image:

'One of the things I like about this company is that you seem to really understand what customers are looking for, and you seem to go the extra mile to help them.'

Q154 What would you say is our organization's greatest weakness?

Be certain of your facts before you open this door. Your background research into the organization should have told you what you need to know, but it might be useful to perform a quick SWOT analysis on what you read – (Strengths, Weaknesses, Opportunities, Threats). When praising strengths, don't over-praise but be reasonably objective. If you talk about weaknesses, make sure they are not criticisms of individuals or teams. A safer response is to talk about external factors: the 'difficult' marketplace or the impact of new technology, then talk about market positioning and ways you might help this organization to gain an advantage. Another technique is to focus on a past weakness:

'I think a weakness in the past has been your difficulties going over to wireless technology. However I see from this week's FT that you've introduced a completely new product range…'

Q155 What is the worst thing you ever heard about our organization?

Depending on the organization, this may be easy or difficult to answer. First of all, the principle of disclosure makes you shine or falter. Let's assume that the organization is in the news with bad press. If you appear *not* to be aware of the news, the interviewer will be lead to believe either that you are not knowledgeable about current events or (and it is hard to tell which is worse) that you do not wish to admit your knowledge. If the law has been broken, and the organization has been found guilty and subject to fines and other penalties, and all this is public knowledge, state what you know. Then listen carefully to the comments the interviewer makes. By doing so you show empathy, and that is appreciated.

If the matter has not been resolved or is a matter of hearsay, be careful and practise answering this question before the interview in the presence of a trusted colleague or two to determine how much to share and withhold. If you have heard gossip and innuendo, repeat not one word. If the worst you have heard is that the competition for jobs at the organization is fierce because it is a terrific company – and you can say it with a straight face – that could be a sharp response.

*Q156 How long will it take for you to make a meaningful contribution to the role?

If you provide too long *a time frame*, interviewers wonder if you will ever make a contribution. Saying '*From day one!*' requires an explanation of what you can do for the organization immediately. Organizations recognize the learning curve that any new employee is expected to undergo. *The higher the level of the person hired, the more tolerant the organization is about expecting quick results*, but in those instances the later the impact, the greater the results. In no case extend the time frame beyond six months, and include some indication of the 'quick wins' you might hope to achieve.

Q157 How fast will you contribute to the organization's success?

This is a variation of the immediately preceding question. It is a little easier to deal with because you can say that you will begin to contribute in small ways from the commencement of your employment. As you grow into your assignment with the organization – and especially after six months – your contributions will grow as well.

Q158 Some people feel that spending too much time in any one position shows a lack of initiative. What is your opinion?

The interviewer may be talking about you. Clarify the point at the beginning of your answer by saying, '*My CV might suggest that to you*'. Then proceed with the response: '*But I do not think it applies because of the variety of challenges I had to face and grew with – until very recently.*' The point is that what constitutes too much time in any position is not a specific length but varies based on the position and the challenges of the position. Never take an interviewer's stated opinion at face value – devil's advocate is just as common.

Q159 What is your present/past employer launching this year?

You may find that one of the reasons you've been called in for interview is to mine you for information about your previous or present employer. Clearly you will have to say something about what your employer has been doing, but some interviewers working for direct competitors will want to take it further. They may use this as an opportunity to persuade you to give away insider information about your employer's weaknesses, product lines, or plans for the future. You should resist attempts to mine you like this. First, you may be breaching a confidentiality agreement, and secondly it gives the impression that you can't keep things to yourself. Reframe the question around your own experience:

'It wouldn't be professional to discuss confidential plans they have for this year, but I can tell you about my contribution to last month's product launch which you will already know about.'

Q160 What did you dislike about your last job?

Preferably identify minor nuisances and inconveniences. Keep in mind that your interviewer is not asking for the purpose of correcting them. Preface your remarks with a comment that, *'For the most part I really liked my job but – as with any job – there were a few minor frustrations'.* Then mention general irritants that, if corrected, would have enabled you (or anyone, really) to work more effectively. Try to stick with only two.

'The computers crashed.'

'The IT system we commissioned wasn't up to our expectations.'

'Salespeople don't pass on correct details of customer requirements.'

'Poor communication between departments.'

'So many people never checked their email.'

You'll notice from the above that your ideal criticisms are (1) general problems that all but the most obtuse manager would agree as limiting performance, and (2) are critical of peers, suppliers, systems or equipment, and *not* critical of superiors or subordinates.

Q161   What is your relationship with your former employer?

'We continue to keep in touch,' is a nice way to start if that is the truth. Sometimes an employer of a departing employee invites the ex-employee back to do consultancy work. If this is true, say so because this scenario suggests a real respect for the applicant, and that message will be heard.

If you haven't kept in contact, don't worry because a continuing relationship with a former employer is, under some circumstances, as difficult to maintain as a relationship with a divorced spouse.

'I keep in touch with many of my former colleagues, but I feel it's healthy to move on.'

Q162   Can you work overtime? Evenings? Weekends? Travel?

Don't be intimidated. Agree if you are willing to do so. *Take the question as an opportunity to talk about the demands of the job rather than your restrictions.* Don't immediately say 'yes' without qualification, but seek details and more information first. It is reasonable to ask some detailed questions about working conditions, rates of pay for overtime, travel allowances, etc. but *save these questions until you are offered the job.* At this stage indicate flexibility:

'As you can see from my work history, I'm happy to travel if the job requires it.'

Portray yourself as someone with a strong work ethic but at the same time not overwhelmed by your work. Do bear in mind that in some organizations it's a black mark if your jacket isn't over your chair at 7pm, while in others flexitime allows even senior managers to leave before 5pm.

Q163   What's your pressure point? What makes you crack?

A very probing interviewer will want to know how you behave under extreme pressure. In fact, everyone has their pressure point. What often happens when we're put under pressure is that certain personality traits become emphasized. If we're naturally irritable, we may become extremely so. If we tend to be gloomy or blame ourselves when things go wrong, these characteristics may also come out.

A recruitment interview is not the time to bare your soul. Everyone, including the person interviewing you, behaves less than perfectly when the heat is on. What you need to do is to convey the impression that you are reasonably robust, expect from time to time to work under pressure, and know roughly how you will react:

'Pressure comes with the job. I work hard and then play hard to let off steam rather than letting my work performance suffer.'

'Under pressure I tend to get very focused on the real issues at hand and try not to get distracted when everyone else is running around like headless chickens.'

*Q164   Everyone on the short list has similar background and experience. Why should we appoint YOU?

You need to briefly give a strong answer. Discuss your skills ('can do') and your motivation ('will do'), relating them specifically to the organization and the position ('fit').

Combine those facts with a comment on your wish to be a part of this organization, and you have given a concise and powerful answer.

'Not only do I have the technical understanding of the software itself but I have the communication skills to show staff and customers how to get the best out of it. I think you'll find someone with my technical skills fairly easily, but you might find it harder to get someone who is capable of translating complex information into everyday language – and retaining customers on the way.'

Q165 Have you ever been denied a salary increase?

A 'yes' portrays you as a person with a problem, regardless of the situation in the organization. Being denied a salary increase is different from just not getting a salary increase. The idea that you have been denied a salary increase when one was requested suggests that you over-estimate your value. Focus on times when you have asked for one and eventually got it. **An unqualified negative reply is always the best and the strongest answer**, but better to qualify that 'no' by indicating times when your bid for a pay rise was successful, and times when you were offered unexpected pay rises.

Q166 Have you ever been asked to take a pay cut? Describe the circumstances.

Although taking a pay cut is different from being denied a pay increase, an explanation is required if you have ever agreed to one. With a pay cut the circumstances may have required your acceptance for the good of the organization. If an equity offer was included (as the airlines have recently been doing), then you are showing yourself to be a person with a reasonable yet long-term view that also expresses faith in (and loyalty to) the organization.

Q167 Have you ever been asked to resign?

Determine in advance how to handle this question if the answer is 'yes'. Admit it to the interviewer, disclosing the circumstances as briefly and objectively as possible. When faced with an ultimatum from an employer, the scar is usually deep and long-lasting (if not permanent). Present an objective spin and demonstrate a firm, confident conviction that you benefited from the experience.

'I was asked to resign at XYZ corporation because there was a major downscale of activities and I was given the choice of taking a position of less responsibility or leaving. If I had taken the lower-level position, there still would have been no guarantee that that job would have any more security. If I had stayed, the severance package may have been less or none at all. So I left. It really worked out well, though, because I quickly found a position at DEF Industries with a 20% pay rise. As you know, XYZ on the other hand shortly after went out of existence and 200 employees were out of work with only unemployment benefits at their disposal.'

As with any other factual responses, be certain that your version is corroborated by your former employer(s) in case a specific reference is taken.

Q168 Have you ever been fired? Describe the circumstances.

Many pieces of research confirm that a high proportion of all terminations are the result of work relationship problems. Remember this when considering your response to this question. The general principle here is to be as positive as you can, and be brief. If it happened, admit it and end with a comment to the effect that, *'I certainly learned from this experience.'*

There are many reasons why a person gets fired, including:

■ *Poor interpersonal relationships with your boss, colleagues, subordinates, your boss's boss.* As mentioned, displaced employees frequently identify poor interpersonal relations as the primary cause for their termination of employment. If this is the reason you left your job, do not share that fact with the interviewer. Even if you firmly believe that relationships with only one type of person will make you an effective employee, best not to disclose it.

Be mindful of the fact that dismissals are usually complex affairs. Even if you feel that your relationship with your boss was the reason you were fired, think about what you are about to disclose and consider the ramifications seriously. If you admit you had a tough time getting along with your boss (who, by the way, may have been the worst boss in the world), that is one thing. If in addition you admit to being fired (as opposed to walking out), then you are admitting to two major facts of disclosure: failure to 'get along' and being fired.

What if you were given the option to resign? Then you can say you resigned. How much more you wish to share is up to you. But if you sound like a problem employee, you will not get the job.

■ *Incompetence.* This is complicated. If you were fired because you could not do the job, how does it sound to the person who is interviewing you? The first question to follow may be, '*Why was this not detected during their selection process?*' Before considering admitting to this one, determine whether the job they are considering you for is similar (or, worse, identical) in responsibility to the one from which you were just fired. The only way out is along the lines of '… *the responsibilities of the position were significantly altered between the time I was hired and the time I started.*' You must then be prepared to give the circumstances surrounding the situation, to briefly describe the events that altered the scope of the position – a restructuring, new technology, the hire or departure of a player who was key to the position you were to occupy, etc.

■ *Lack of work or redundancy.* This is a common occurrence today and is easily accepted by potential employers. Usually employers feel that they and other organizations try to save their best employees regardless of the situation. If you lost your job because the position was made redundant, be careful not to use the word 'fired'. Talk about the number of other people who were made redundant at the same time. Using terms like *'redundant,' 'laid off,' 'given a severance package'* are all euphemisms that say *the loss of your job was due not to your performance but to circumstances beyond your control.*

■ *Other reasons* including constructive dismissal, bullying at work, sexual harassment or unlawful discrimination. A word of advice: never mention to a future employer that you lost your most recent job because of some action that might have led to an industrial tribunal. If you do disclose any such thing, the interviewer is highly likely to dismiss you as a candidate. Recruiters react very badly to candidates who are perceived as being potential adversaries in a future legal battle.

Q169 Describe an occasion where your work was criticized.

This is a probing question raised by an experienced (and/or well trained) interviewer. The answer you provide offers the interviewer an opportunity to consider:

■ *Your ability to communicate effectively* with a situation that is extremely personal yet at the same time totally professional.
■ Your *tolerance* for criticism.

- The *scope* of your activities and projects.
- The level of your *participation* in those activities and projects.
- The *environment* in which you have been working.

All this from this one non-hostile, open question!

Ideally, consider describing situations that show your work was criticized but portraying it as borne out by the situation itself. Also consider 'grey area' situations because usually your judgment is not being assessed as wrong and the interviewer can recognize that, in some instances, a risk has to be taken. Refer to your **Experience Worksheet** and **Critical Incidents Worksheet (Chapter 10)** to refresh your memory.

Here are some sample responses:

'Last year we had a really big snowstorm and I made it a point to get in early – I knew there would be a lot of problems to deal with. Many of us got in because the worst of the snow came mid-morning. In an effort to thank all the employees who had bothered to show up for work (and keep up morale), I recommended to management that all employees at work be invited to use the cafeteria for lunch that day at no cost. The MD wondered about the soundness of the proposal and felt it was over-generous and encouraged the idea that coming into work was above and beyond the call of duty. It was no big deal, and I accepted their decision.'

'We were under a great deal of pressure to meet the deadline on a project to install payroll software, and it needed to be done by the end of the year. In a project meeting that no one wanted to attend, the technical people would not offer a target date for the completion of the installation. Since they wouldn't, I did. After the meeting I learned that they complained to my boss and were incensed that I was so 'heavy-handed.' The project was completed on the date that I had projected, and we all went on to complete several more important projects after that with very little altercation ever again.'

By now you are getting the idea. If, however, you are able to recall only a situation in which your work was criticized, begin with a caveat that it was never a major matter (unless it really was and even then don't emphasize it). Then, when you provide a brief scenario, don't choose one where you really made a major error of poor judgement. Also try to select a situation in which, even though initially you were over-ruled, sooner or later good judgement and your insight prevailed. The only thing left is not to hammer the point home at the expense of your adversaries. Try to show win-win. If you didn't win, it was no big deal for you and it is best to convey the impression that you did not take it personally.

Q170 What question could I ask that would really intimidate you?

This is one of the most terrible questions to deal with because it puts applicants to a test that requires a most demanding answer. Once you state the question, the interviewer then asks the question that he or she would not have thought of asking in the first place.

When preparing in advance for this question, consider all the questions that may come up so that this question from the interviewer is just an opportunity to answer another one. The only difference is that the burden is on you not only to provide a question but also to be ready with an answer.

However, there is an alternative: choose a question that the interviewer has already asked. This accomplishes two things. First, your answer flatters the interviewer, who has already come up with what you consider to be a really intimidating question! Second, by identifying a question already asked, you do not have to answer a tough question that the interviewer had not considered. You do not have to add to the arsenal. Again, you can also take the opportunity to slip in a question for which you have a strong answer.

Q171   If our roles were reversed, what questions would you ask?

If you are ready for this question, usually only one question is required. Ask the question that you feel is most relevant and also affords you the opportunity to give a strong, positive confident answer. Do not for a second consider a question that comments in any way on your possible inappropriateness for the position and/or organization being discussed. The answer *'You have already covered all the questions very thoroughly'* or something to that effect is weak.

If you feel strong with preparation, suggest either *'What can you do for us?'* or *'What makes you think you want to join our organization?'* These questions tell the interviewer you are a confident person and are willing to answer questions that others may consider intimidating. *This is also a chance to slip in a question that you really want to be asked because you have an excellent response* that can advance your candidacy.

Q172   What skills or requirements do you think your boss should have in this position?

If you know enough about the position to feel qualified to answer, go ahead. In the process, be sure to emphasize the skills and qualities that you possess. If necessary, briefly mention other skills that are required and that you may complement or support. Then be silent.

Q173   Where does your boss think you are right now?

This is a nasty question to ask an applicant who is currently in a job. Don't use it as an excuse to vent your feelings about your boss (*'I don't know and I don't care'*). Communicating disloyalty and a willingness to deceive will not endear you to a potential employer. Equally important is to avoid being caught in a lie:

'I arranged to take some leave/free time/flexitime.'

'I rearranged my lunch hour to make this appointment.'

'Since I came in early this morning to clear up my desk, I explained to my supervisor that I had a personal matter to attend to this afternoon.'

Q174 What will you say in your resignation letter if we offer you this job?

This again, is probing your motivation to change jobs. Remember that a number of candidates get to job offer stage and then turn down the offer. As the discussion around **Q55** suggests, there is always some pressure on candidates if their present employer makes a counter-offer.

Another critical step is sitting down to write a resignation letter, and then actually handing it in. Interviewers probe this to see if your motivation to change jobs is genuine, or if you are a 'time waster' and taking interviews just to check your market worth.

'I'd state very simply that I had enjoyed my time with the company and was moving on to new things. And I'd thank them for giving me a really interesting opportunity.'

Q175 How long would you stay with us?

You need to think right answer/wrong answer for this 'gotcha' question. Think about it. If you switched roles with your inter-viewer, what would you want to hear? Consider the organiza-tion you are meeting with and the 'time lines' they consider appropriate. If you are meeting with a highly entrepreneurial company, you do not want to say something along the lines of '*I am looking for a place to stay until I retire.*' In most cases, the security-tinged tone of the answer will not be well received. Sometimes, however, circumstances can make this answer appropriate even in an entrepreneurial environment. If, for instance, you are nearing retirement age that would be a most effective answer regardless of organization because it tells the employer that there is a specific limit to your stay. At the same time you both know your intent up front.

Consider and try to determine the 'right' answer with your interviewer in mind, but be careful not to say something that would reflect inconsistencies with the rest of your presentation. '*I have never been a job hopper. I'd like to be in a role with a long-term future.*'

✳Q176 What do we have to do to keep you challenged?

'*As long as I continue to learn*' is a troublesome reply because the tone suggests that the organization is responsible for your well-being and you have now established a problem. The burden on the employer (if they hire you) is to constantly worry that you feel that you are always learning. Employers want applicants who bring solutions with them; they have enough problems already.

In a 'paternal' organization, the culture is family-like. That is, you are carefully and constantly oriented to the organization, and the organization tries to do it effectively by blurring the lines between personal and professional. If it is a style you prefer and you see that as the organization's approach, say, '*I plan be here for the long term – that is, of course, if the organization permits.*' Then explain that you see work as an opportunity to 'belong' and that belonging to this great organization would be quite a coup.

Q177 Why are you interested in coming to work in this town?

The interviewer is asking this question in order to find out how far you are motivated to move house or work in a new location.

Regardless of the location, *part of the job search process should include research on the location of the organization* where it seems most likely that you will be working. Keep your comments confined to the specific question. Suppose the location is not the most desirable, such as an inner city area ripe for urban renewal or a boring industrial park. Make the point that the reason for your interest in the location is particularly due to the opportunities presented by the organization, which has chosen to set up shop there.

Q178 Why aren't you earning more at your age?

Another terrible question. Do not succumb. Do not challenge the premise.

'When I was just out of university I considered other factors besides pay as being more important. I should have paid more attention to my career in my early years. That is exactly why we are having this meeting.'

An alternative is to demonstrate that your career choices have been active rather than passive:

'Yes, I've looked at a number of better-paid roles, but I decided that the company I was with offered me far better training opportunities than I could get anywhere else. Now that I am fully qualified, however, I want to be paid the going rate for the job.'

Q179 Why would someone with your experience want to work *here*?

If this question is asked openly, it is very straightforward – back to matching your skills and qualities with the needs of the job.

However, sometimes an unprofessional interviewer will put you off balance with a question that appears to be a subversive comment about the organization itself. Don't be drawn into any kind of criticism of the organization, stated or implied.

In some organizations there is an air of bitterness or cynicism, often if there has recently been a round of downsizing. *Listen but do not participate, regardless of your feelings.* If you are subjected to a disgruntled employee's monologue during the recruitment and selection process, listen and keep your distance. You may win in two ways. First, a job offer may be coming your way because the person speaking to you liked you enough to open up without fear of – or concern for – retribution. Second, you are getting deep insight into the organization from an insider – great data for you to consider while deciding whether you are interested in accepting a job if it is offered.

Q180 You've met the boss earlier today. Do you really think you could work for someone like that?

Again, this may be open cynicism or a test to draw you out. The only way to answer is to be slightly naive and take the question entirely at face value without referring to any implied criticism.

Q181 Would you like to have my job?

Don't be tempted to respond, '*Only for the next 10 minutes so that I could hire myself.*' Be direct and say, '*With all the chal-*

lenges in the position I am being considered for, I will certainly be kept busy for quite a while'.

Q182   What reservations do you have about working here?

If you have any, now is not the time to raise them. As far as this interviewer is concerned, the job should seem ideal to you. Quash the temptation to say something like, '*I only hope that I am good enough to make it here.*' Instead, say:

'I see this position as a fine opportunity and the organization as one I would be proud to join. I don't have any reservations – it all sounds very interesting.'

Q183   May I have your business card?

If you have portrayed yourself as a consultant, you need to have a good quality business card – the quality of the card (texture, logo, print) are all part of the statement that you are making. Having a personal business card may not be such a good idea if you are applying for permanent positions – it rather looks as if you haven't decided whether you want to be self-employed or not. If you are in a job and you don't want to give out your business contact number, perhaps best just to provide a CV.

Q184   If you were going to Mars, what three things would you take?

Believe it or not, this question comes up from time to time. One reason may be to challenge your creativity. Another is to determine how you act under pressure. This is a fantasy question – in other words, it has nothing to do with the job in question and is used either just to be clever or to throw you off balance. Don't let the question floor you even if it really bothers you – don't let the interviewer see that you are easily rattled. Best not to take the answer too seriously:

'Oh, it's one of those questions. Let me see. A good book. A clockwork torch to read with in case the light failed. And a map of Mars, perhaps. What would you take?'

Other equally pointless questions that might trouble you include:

- If you were an animal in the jungle, what kind of animal would you be?
  'The biggest one.'
- What's the best way to nail jelly to a ceiling?
  'Patiently.'

Q185 Sell me this paper clip.

If you've applied to be a bookkeeper, this is still a fantasy question, but if your role involves selling, it's not unusual for the interviewer to ask you to demonstrate your powers of influence and persuasion. Don't duck the question, and practise some techniques in advance. One simple sales technique is to quickly get your target to say 'yes' as many times as possible – 'yes' to the need for a paper clip, 'yes' to the fact that it will make his life easier, 'yes' to the fact that *this* paper clip is both useful and attractive and 'yes' to your proposition that it's excellent value for money. Play it tongue in cheek, but play to win.

Stress Reduction Techniques

- **Prepare ahead of time**. What are your weaknesses? What are your professional sore spots? Accept your lack of perfection and look for what you can do to compensate.
- Avoid going on the defensive.
- Try taking the offensive and turn the situation around. Answer a question with a question. ('Has this been a major problem?')
- **Keep your cool**. Sweating, fidgeting, grimaces and eye-rolling send messages of acute discomfort (or worse), which may be interpreted by the interviewer as 'has something to hide' or 'cannot handle this interview – how can he or she handle the job?'.
- **Slow it down**. Don't blurt out an answer just to move on to another topic. Speak calmly.
- **Appear to welcome probing questions**. If you appear uncomfortable, the interviewer knows that it's time to probe further.
- When in doubt as to what response to make, take an unnoticeable deep breath, pause, and try for as confident and sincere an answer as you can offer.

13

Unlawful and Unethical Questions

QUESTIONS YOU SHOULDN'T HAVE TO ANSWER

How the law protects interviewees

This is not the place to discuss in detail the restrictions which the law imposes on interviewers. You will be aware of many of them. While HR professionals and recruiters can work with the law on the basis of 'I'll look it up when I need it', they need to keep some knowledge in the forefront of their minds while asking questions in selection interviews.

In general, the principle of UK recruitment law is that an employer is required to choose the right person for the job, and not to discriminate unfairly on several grounds, which include race, racial origin, sex, marital status, disability, and trade union membership. Legislation is on its way which may also outlaw discrimination on the grounds of age or religious belief. In addition, there are codes of practice which encourage employers to operate fair and open selection policies.

Having said that – employers still 'discriminate' in the true sense of the word – i.e. 'choosing'. There is no law in the UK which requires employers to fulfil any kind of quota or to force employers to select a person because of his or her gender, ethnicity – or indeed any other factor which is not directly related to an individual's ability to do the job. What an employer *may not do* is discriminate against employees and applicants on the basis of any category protected by law. Employers may still ask irrelevant (to the applicant) questions as long as they do not touch on categories defined and protected by this law. If, however, a worker takes an employer to an Industrial Tribunal, a recruiter will in general terms have to *demonstrate from records* that the selection decision was made fairly.

Why Do Interviewers Ask Illegal Questions?

■ **They may be asked out of ignorance**. Employment legislation gets more complex every year. If the interviewer is not a trained HR or recruitment specialist, mistakes may be made.

■ **They may be asked out of arrogance**. A certain strange group of people try to raise illegal issues. For odd reasons they feel the need to test authority. They are going to ask anything they 'damn well please,' and no human resource professional and, for that matter, no one else is going to stop them. To make their point, persons with this attitude take any recruitment and selection opportunity to ask illegal and other inappropriate questions. Thankfully, this kind of dinosaur is now a fairly rare beast.

■ **They may be asked out of innocence**. Poor interviewers are those who have had little or no training. They may even have had the training and/or experience, but they do not have the proficiency required to interview effectively. The problem may also stem from the fact that they had no or little time to prepare for the interview. Whatever the reason, these persons frequently try to impress themselves with the ease with which they are able to ask questions. Yet they do not realize that the key to effective interviewing is not thinking about the next question but rather concentrating on the answers. As a result, when these persons realize that they have run out of questions but feel they are not ready to close the meeting, they blurt out an illegal or high-risk question. These interviewers may be intimidated by the applicant and seek to find common ground (children of the same ages, similar religions) in an effort to put themselves more at ease.

What to Say When Asked an Illegal or Inappropriate Question

First of all, you may consider answering the question and getting on with the interview. This is a judgement call. You aren't the recruitment expert here, and pulling an interviewer up on a question which you may feel is illegal will almost certainly destroy any rapport that exists.

What if the interviewer persists with the illegal questions? Firstly, it's very difficult for you without a detailed knowledge of law and good practice to know whether an interview question is just a poor question, is a question which an employer is not recommended to ask, or is plain unlawful. You may decide to make a note of the question and pursue the matter via a tribunal. This is your right. It could tie up a great deal of your time and energy, but it will at least encourage an employer to take the law seriously.

A compromise position is not to challenge the question (after all, you may not be 100% sure if the question is illegal) and to reframe it through your answer. The following questions are unlawful or inadvisable. Each requires a diplomatic answer that brings the focus back to work.

Q186   How would you fit in here in an all-white workforce?

Almost certainly an illegal question as it appears that the selection decision will indirectly discriminate against workers who are not white. This situation sometimes arises where an employer normally recruits only by word of mouth, and has been required to open out recruitment that is more representative of the community. Your answer should focus on the job, not the context.

'I get on with most people as long as they do a good job and pull their weight.'

Q187 Who will look after your children while you are at work?

This question may be illegal, depending on whether it's asked of all applicants or only women. It's certainly very poor practice and appears to indicate a bias against women. You may choose not to answer, or to indicate that you find the question uncomfortable or discriminatory. If you choose to answer, once again focus on the needs of the job. The precise details of how you propose to manage childcare are not the concern of your employer.

'I have children, and they are important to me, but I have always managed both a home and a job. What is the commitment here in terms of travel and nights away from home?'

'My track record clearly shows that I've always managed to work whatever hours are required. What are your hours of work here?'

Q188 Do you plan to have children?

An illegal question, almost without doubt, especially as it will almost certainly only be asked of women. Sometimes employers are concerned that they may have to pay Maternity Pay, and at other times the interviewer is checking out how committed workers will be in the long term. Again, it's highly likely that you will want to object to such a question.

'As you know, that's a question I don't have to answer. However I can give you a clear indication that I am firmly committed to having a long-term career in this field.'

Q189 Why should I hire someone who's been out of the labour market for 10 years?

Clearly, as this question is most likely to be addressed to women who have taken time off to raise children, it is probably unlawful and certainly unacceptable. However, although an employer cannot discriminate unfairly against women returners, you don't get any special advantage – you still need to be able to prove that you can do the job.

'You're probably concerned that I don't have the latest IT skills. I can tell you that I've recently attended a refresher course. I've also done most of the paperwork for our local golf club for the last two years using all the latest software. I think my skills are pretty up to date.'

Q190 Do you have any dependants at home that you look after?

Unacceptable, probably illegal. An employer should select you because you can do the job, and not make assumptions about limitations on your working commitment that may arise from looking after children, elderly relatives, or anyone else. Same answer as **Q187**.

Q191 This job requires long hours. Will this be a problem for your spouse and/or your children?

'I'm not comfortable with this question, but I think what you really want to know is whether I have any restrictions on working normal hours of work. I don't.'

Genuine Occupational Qualifications

You may occasionally come across jobs which specifically ask for a person of a particular sex or race. While the job ads could simply be illegal, there is also a chance that the job in question is a particular kind of exception to legislation controlling sex and race discrimination. There may be a Genuine Occupational Qualification (GOQ) involved. There are a small number of grounds which can be summarized as *authenticity, decency* and *welfare*. Simple examples would include:

- A female actress to play the part of Lady Bracknell.
- A black male actor to play the part of Othello.
- A male or female changing-room attendant.
- A female rape counsellor.
- A live-in carer with one or more clients of the same sex.
- A person of a particular ethnic background to work in a community centre.

Note, however, that these jobs are fairly rare and, where they are advertised, there is usually a very clear statement of the fact that a Genuine Occupational Qualification has been established.

Inappropriate Questions Which May (or May Not) be Unlawful

Q192 Where were you born?

This is unlikely to be relevant to the job. If the question is *'Are you eligible to work in this country?'* that is reasonable. Indeed, under current legislation an employer is responsible for checking that applicants are legally entitled to work in the UK. Best to give a quick answer and see where the questions lead.

Q193 That is an interesting accent. What country are you from? What country are your parents from? You have an unusual last name. Where do you come from?

Other variations may include: 'What is your native language?' 'What language do you speak at home?'

Interviewers may raise such questions either because they have run out of questions or because they are truly curious.

These questions may be a form of indirect indiscrimination since the only issues are (a) whether you can do the job and (b) whether you are legally entitled to hold a job in the UK (through being a British subject, for example, or holding a valid work permit). It's best to answer simply, but make it clear that you are uncomfortable with the questions.

'I was brought up in Manchester.' 'I speak English, just like you.'

Q194   Which country did you qualify in?

It's a form of indirect discrimination in the UK to ask specifically for degrees or other qualifications obtained in the UK. However, some professions have detailed rules about the equivalence and acceptability of qualifications gained in other countries. Make enquiries of the appropriate professional bodies if this is an issue.

Q195   Are you married? How would your husband feel about you taking this job?

This is a grey area question. On the face of it, it may not be illegal to ask the question, provided that you ask it of both men and women applicants. However, it's potentially a minefield question, and can have no bearing on the applicant's ability to do the job. Discrimination on marital grounds is covered by the Sex Discrimination Act, and such questions rarely have any real bearing on the job in question.

Q196   Do you have any previous convictions?

An employer is entitled to ask this question, and you are obliged to answer. If your convictions are 'spent' under the terms of the Rehabilitation of Offenders Act, you can legally say 'no' – unless the job is specifically exempted. This should be made clear well before you go into an interview.

Q197   You haven't worked in years. What makes you think you are up to the challenges of the position and our organization?

This question is potentially discriminatory because it will probably be asked more of women returners than of other job seekers.

'While I have not been in paid employment for several years, I have had to perform a variety of activities and play a number of roles for projects in the ____ sector. Let me give you an example of skills that I have developed that I am certain will be most useful to you here. For example, I supervised the automation of the XYZ Charity, that brought the organization into the information age and did it while expanding fund-raising efforts.'

Q198   Don't you think you're a little old for this job?

It's not illegal for an employer to ask for your age or your date of birth. However it's poor practice to make selection decisions on the basis of age, and may shortly be illegal.

You can't keep your age a secret in the recruitment process. The best plan is to simply include your date of birth on the last page of your CV, and don't make anything further of it. If the issue comes up in interview, play to your strengths:

'I think I have maturity and experience that younger applicants are missing. Besides, they'll be off in 2 years, whereas I'm looking for a long-term position.'

Q199   How can you do this job with your disability?

It is perfectly legal for an employer to ask you whether you are disabled on an application form or in an interview. In fact, in law it's up to the job-seeker to declare any kind of disability. A 'disability' as far as recruitment is concerned is usually a long-term health problem or condition that limits your employ-ability in some way. It is illegal to make a selection decision which discriminates against those with disabilities, and employers are also obliged to make adjustments to the recruit-ment and selection processes in order to allow access to disabled candidates (e.g. special facilities for visually impaired candidates taking tests, or wheelchair access to interview rooms). Employers are also able to receive government funding to make adjustments to the workplace to allow and encourage disabled job-seekers to find work. The law in this area is complex, and operates around what is 'reasonable' for an employer. If you are a disabled job-seeker, take specialist advice and keep abreast of updates by reading the excellent *Disability Rights Handbook*, published annually by the Disability Alliance.

Dealing with Illegal Questions

- Interviewers should not ask them and you do not have to answer.
- In all circumstances **you can control the amount of disclo-sure** when faced with an illegal question. If the truth of the matter can help your candidacy, consider offering the information.
- Try to reframe the question rather than answering it directly or challenging the questioner. One colludes, one confronts.
- Interviewers or organizations that insist on asking illegal ques-tions or have a **bias based on sex, race, national origin, ethnic origin or disability may be doing you a favour** in revealing their colours early in the interview process.
- Even though it is disappointing and frustrating to be asked illegal and/or inappropriate questions, **do not allow *your* professionalism to slip**.

- **Questions are illegal whether asked orally or on an application form if asked before you are offered the job**. However, questions on health, age, gender and marital status may be on application forms – as long as the information is not used to decide who to appoint.
- In the worst of cases, **to follow up and make a claim of discrimination** against an organization that asks illegal questions, contact your local Jobcentre or Citizens Advice Bureau.
- Remember that you also have legal obligations. Any information you include in an application form must be honest. If it isn't, your employer may have grounds to dismiss you without notice.

The Wrap-up

AND FINALLY ...

✳Q200 Do you have any questions for us?

Too many candidates politely say, '*No, you've covered everything in great detail, thank you.*' Wrong answer! Say this, and interviewers feel that you have insufficient interest in the job and just want to get home and do something more interesting.

'*Yes, I do have a question. How is the job likely to change in the next couple of years?*'

Why You Should Ask Questions

Since an interview is a two-way conversation with a purpose, applicants should also ask questions. A well-balanced interview gives both parties sufficient information to come to a decision – the interviewer decides if you fit the role, and you decide whether the organization is right for you. The questions *you* ask during the interview are important.

Before every interview, as part of the preparation, think up three or four questions you feel you may be able to ask at the end. Don't have too many, but line up a small selection. This way, if one or two questions are already covered during the interview, you have at least one good question left.

Your questions should be written down before the meeting. Try to keep them short and simple so that you can remember them by just glancing at your notes. Better still, draw a symbol on the edge of the job description to remind you of the question topic. Don't read the question aloud from notes – it sounds as if you haven't really listened to anything that's gone on during the interview. Make it as spontaneous as possible.

Resist taking more than a very occasional note during an employment interview. You might make one or two. That said, how do you remember the answers to the questions you raised? You should debrief yourself immediately after each and every interview, recording the key things you learned. The primary reason is that we all forget more than 60% of anything we have been told within three days after hearing it. The sooner after the meeting you review the answers, the better the chance you have of retaining the correct answers.

The following looks at different kinds of questions you will have in mind before, during and after the job interview.

Establishing the Facts

Before the interview, no matter how good your research, you'll have a number of unanswered questions. These are not necessarily the questions you will use at the end of the interview.

Most basic questions can be answered by a visit to the company's website and a read through the latest annual report – and you will have covered these in detail to answer the questions in **Chapter 2**. You may however have to ask some of these in the interview itself (for example if it is a small or new organization that has little information available about it in the public arena), e.g.:

- *'Who owns the company?'*
- *'Where can I find out more about your product range?'*

Some questions will help you to know how the selection process will be concluded:

- *'Who will make the final selection decision?'*
- *'How soon do you want an employee in place? When will the appointment decision be made?'*

Don't waste the valuable moments at the end of the interview finding out things that can be discussed at job offer stage. Remember that you can find a great deal of information about the company from other sources:

- From staff on reception.
- From members of the department.
- From staff who used to work in the company.
- From suppliers, external consultants, sister or parent organizations.
- From other industry or professional contacts.

Questions to Help you Decide Whether you Want the Job

You may also want to ask some questions to confirm whether the job is exactly what you think it is. These questions may help you to decide whether to accept a job offer. Some organizations will consciously 'sell' themselves to you during the interview, others will tell you the barest facts.

Bear in mind that the interview itself may not be a great moment to establish small points of detail, like exactly where you will fit on the salary scale, when the next pay review is, or what mileage rate the company pays for travel. However, the interview may be the only face-to-face meeting you'll get with one of the key decision-makers in the organization, so this is certainly a good opportunity to **ask** and **seek flexibility**.

Ask about areas of job content that need clarifying:

'Would I be responsible for bringing in new business?'

'What training and learning opportunities are available?'

If you feel that the job is almost the perfect fit but needs a little tailoring, you may (particularly with more senior positions) get a chance to seek some **flexibility**, e.g.:

'How open would you be to me delegating some of the process parts of this job and initiating some new projects to add to the income stream?'

Some questions are appropriate for more senior appointments, e.g.:

'How committed are you to introducing new technology within the next 12 months?'

'Do you expect your recent rate of income/sales increase/decline to continue this year?'

'Who exactly controls the marketing budget?'

'When is this project likely to come on line, and what happens if it doesn't?'

(Note, however, that this kind of question might be left until after you've received a job offer. It depends how many buying signals the interviewer is giving you and how easy it will be to gain access to this decision-maker again after the interview is over.)

Questions to Make You Shine

The questions you ask at the end of the interview are there for one purpose only: **to give you a last, memorable opportunity to shine.** We looked at the effect of first impressions in **Chapter 4** – remember, too, that the final things you say will also have a lasting impact, particularly if you are the last candidate of the day.

Before you ask any questions at the end of the interview, **say something positive** about the role. That's because there's a chance that the overall message behind your question is that you are not sure whether you want the job or not. At this stage, this could be a reason to exclude you. Ask your questions, but preface them with a positive comment: *'First of all I'd like to say how interesting this job sounds. I just want to clarify one or two things.'*

'I've got some ideas about developing this department, but before pitching them in I'd just like to ask you how you see its future...'

'Given time, I'd be really interested in helping out with planning the annual conference. Do you think I might be able to have some role in that?'

'I've a number of useful contacts in the publishing business. How would you feel about extending our consultancy services to that sector?'

'One thing I'd really like to add to this role is the prospect of building up a formal mentoring programme. How would you react to that?'

In summary, you won't get the chance to ask more than a couple of questions at the end of an interview. If one or two pop up during the meeting, take your cue from the interviewer as to the topic. Your main chance is however at the end, and the main purpose of your questions is **message reinforcement not information gathering**.

There are really two kinds of questions that work well at the end of the interview.

(a) **Questions that ask about the future of the job, e.g.:**
   'How is the job likely to change in the next 2 years or so?'
   'What learning opportunities is this job likely to offer?'
   'What kinds of clients would I be working with?'

(b) **Questions that focus on the challenge of the job, e.g.:**
'What kind of results would you expect me to achieve in the first 6 months?'
'What would you say I will learn as a result of this job?'

These questions have several effects. They communicate your serious interest in the job, and provide you with some vital insights into the role. However, what they also do is to *create a strong mental picture in the interviewer's mind* – a picture of you doing the job. This could make the difference between being number 2 and number 1 on the shortlist. Once the interviewer has a strong mental image of you actually in the post, it's difficult to shake it off.

Questions to check next steps

You have reached the end of the interview. If it has gone well you have communicated a clear series of points about the way your strengths match the requirements of the job. You have thanked the interviewer for his or her time and for all the information.

An interviewer should give you clear information about what happens next. You should be very clear about this point, and, if not, ask a quick question before you leave the interview room. Will someone contact you, or do you have to ring? When are you likely to hear? When will the interviews finish? Is there a second round of interviews? When will the final decision be taken? Be clear, and write down this information. If you don't hear within the predicted time frame, allow a day's grace, and then ring up to ask where things are up to.

Pitfalls when asking questions

Does raising certain questions put you at risk? Remember that when you ask questions, you are still presenting a picture of yourself. So, yes, there can be a risk. *The burden is on you to determine what question to ask, how to ask it, and most importantly, when.*

Questions at the end of the interview to *avoid*

- Don't ask questions that show that you don't really have a clue what the job is about.
- Don't ask questions that could have been answered by five minutes spent looking at the company website: e.g. 'What exactly do you make here?', 'How many people work here?', 'How many offices do you have?'.
- Don't ask about how flexible the company may be on pay. This is the wrong moment, and could provide a reason to exclude you. Deal with this if and when you're offered the job.
- Don't ask a question that the interviewer is almost certainly unable to answer, or any other question that may embarrass, such as by introducing information about the company unknown to the interviewer.
- Don't be smart, ironic, or try to get your own back for all the probing, difficult, fantasy or unethical questions early on.
- Don't ask for special consideration, apologize, or beg...

Handling Second Interviews

Much of the material included in this book will assist you when it comes to second or third interviews. Remember that in a recruitment process involving more than one interview with an organization, the function of the first interview is generally to establish whether you cover the basic criteria. Subsequent interviews will usually probe your experience, your achievements and your weak points in far more depth.

They will also try to gain more detailed information about organizational 'fit'.

If you are invited back for a second interview, review carefully all the topics that came up in the first meeting. What important issues have yet to be discussed? If you were interviewing for this post, what detailed questions would you ask? Also, think about the responses you have already given in interview. Notes may have been taken. Assuming they were, which of your answers will be probed?

Don't be surprised, however, if the person conducting a second interview has only partial information about what has already been said. Be prepared to repeat your evidence and your Presentation Statements if necessary.

The Job Offer

You've undertaken an effective job search and conducted yourself well in the interview. You've managed not to talk yourself out of the job. You've probably received a number of strong 'buying signals' from the decision-maker (talking about the future, picturing you in the role, telling you why you are a good match, asking when you can start …).

Your First Response

Handling a job offer well takes a little thinking. Job offers are often made verbally, either face-to-face or over the telephone. If the offer is made face-to-face in front of a witness, it may be legally binding. Remember that no matter how much of a hurry the employer is in to offer you the job, you are under no obligation to accept immediately. The danger is that the offer sometimes quickly includes a financial offer: 'I'm delighted to say that we're going to offer you this job. The terms and conditions will be the standard ones. I assume that's OK with you. When can you start?'

The danger is that in your delight to receive a job offer you say 'yes' to everything. However the last thing you want to do is to sound suspicious or under-committed. As with questions you raise during the interview, top and tail your comments with positive remarks.

'I'm delighted with your offer. I really enjoyed our discussion and I know I am really going to enjoy this job. Can you give me a day or so to have a look through the details – perhaps you could send me a draft of your written offer? As for a start date – I'm on three months' notice, but I will see what I can do. I really want to get on with it!'

Continuing your enquiries after a job offer

You may still have questions about the job and the organization. The interview doesn't need to be the last and only opportunity you will have to gather information about critical information for your decision-making process. Too many candidates feel that the only time they are allowed to ask questions about the job is during the selection process. Far from it.

If you get a job offer, it's very reasonable to ask to go back to have a look around the organization, spend some time with the department where your job is based, or to have a real get-to-know-you meeting with your boss (and, ideally, your boss's boss). Ask to spend a day in the company, or at minimum a couple of hours. It shows strong interest on your behalf, but will also help you to decide if you are going to take the job offer.

Negotiating the Financial Offer

Q201 How much would it take to get you? What sort of pay figure did you have in mind?

(a) Answering this question during the interview process

This question can of course come up at any stage in the interview process. Generally, try to keep off the topic of pay until there is a firm job offer on the table. That way you have far more negotiating power. If you've already established the salary you are prepared to accept, you've little room for manoeuvre now. If the question is raised early, such as anytime in the first interview, you may respond by saying, '*I really don't know enough about the job yet to work out what it would pay in the marketplace. What salary range is on offer?*'

Do your homework: Try to find out the answer to this question as early as possible from job advertisements for similar positions, information garnered in other interviews, recruiters, 'inside' information from other employees, or industry research. Work out what the top 10% of earners in this kind of role are earning, and what evidence you need to present to get an offer in that pay range.

(b) Answering this question at the job offer stage

You're in a much better position answering this question when a job offer is already in your possession – ideally one in writing. Now you have some power. The golden rule here is: **only negotiate when the employer has decided you are the one.**

Don't forget that the package is a mix of benefits (bonus and incentive payments, pension contribution, medical insurance, subsidized travel loans, etc.). Negotiate on the things that matter to you.

You may have no idea at all from the job advertisement or from the interview what kind of pay package may be on offer. In a sense, that gives you an advantage, particularly if the interviewer has established what you have been paid in the past.

When it comes to naming a pay figure, always try to get the employer to shoot first:

'What sort of pay range is available for this position?'

Then consider a couple of softening-up questions:

'Is there any flexibility at the top end of the range?'

'Bearing in mind that I'm being interviewed for positions paying around £X, what flexibility is there?'

Other phrases you can use to justify the pay you want:

'I'm being interviewed for positions paying around £X, and I'm not really comfortable about accepting anything lower than that.'

'From what I know of the marketplace, I think good people in this field are earning between £X and £Y. I think I'm worth a salary close to £Y because ... '

'I realize you need to control all your costs, but do bear in mind that I'll make a significant difference to your overall income. We're discussing a salary difference of £5000 a year, and I could easily be bringing you in that much extra income a week.'

(For more details on negotiating pay, a pay rise, or a promotion, see John Lees' *How To Get The Perfect Promotion.*)

Other aspects of the job offer to evaluate

Look at the job offer in the light of these general questions:

■ Will this job enhance your CV? How will it help or hinder the way you present yourself to a recruiter in five years' time?

■ Have you done this kind of job before? If so, what's new about it?
■ What will you learn in this job?
■ How long will the job keep you interested?
■ Can you work with your boss – and your boss's boss?

Thinking about whether the job is the right job is not a counsel of perfection, but a chance to compare two wish lists: what you want in your next career move, and what an employer is looking for. A good match means success for both parties. A poor match means an under-performing employee, another career transition, and an unhappy employer.

What will make the job right will be more than just the salary package, and may include all or some of the points set out in the **Job Offer Checklist** below.

Job Offer Checklist

Give each factor a score as follows:

0 (no match to my wish list)
1 Poor match to my wish list
2 Fair match to my wish list
3 Good match to my wish list

Distance from home		Medical facilities	
Travel time/cost		Sports or entertaining facilities	
Location – city centre or greenfield site			
Public transport route		Travel opportunities/ restrictions	
Pleasant building/ working conditions		Close to other facilities	
Crèche facilities/ assistance		Size of company	

Organizational culture		Performance-related bonuses	
Corporate values		Car/car allowance and running costs	
Community involvement		Profit sharing or share options	
Team fit		Pension plan – contributory or not?	
Relationship with peers		Subsidized loans	
Relationship with boss(es)		Holiday entitlement	
Working hours		Private health scheme	
Status, responsibility, power		Life or incapacity Insurance	
Job content		Relocation costs	
Promotion prospects		Expense account	
On-going training and development		Staff purchase options	
Job security		Telephone/home-working allowances	
Salary/benefits package		Other (define your own)	
Base salary			
Period of review			

When you have completed the Job Offer Checklist, look at the scores you have given and think about the things that matter to you. Is the overall balance right for you? Don't expect everything that matters to have a 3 – but don't believe that this job offer will be the only one you'll ever get.

If a Job Offer Isn't Forthcoming

If you don't get a job offer, don't be disheartened. If you got that close it means you are very employable, but someone is slightly more employable than you – or maybe is a better organizational fit. Remember that you can't control all the factors in the process.

Don't give up. Job interviews are like sales prospects – a number of people have to say 'no' before somebody says 'yes'.

Do try, however, to get some **feedback** on how you did. This will almost certainly only be given to you verbally. Asking *'May I have a couple of pointers on my interview technique?'* may make all the difference to your next interview.

A 10-Step Guide To Pulling Yourself up By Your Bootstraps

What To Do If You Don't Get An Offer

1. Try to learn from your interview experience. Ask for feedback – telephone (the company is very unlikely to spell out their recruitment decision-making process in writing).
2. Focus on what went well in the interview, and build on it.
3. If you intend to go for other jobs in the same industry, get some more practice.
4. Practise, in particular, answers to difficult questions.
5. Work hard on pre-packaging your evidence.
6. Compose your presentation statements. Write them down.
7. Revisit your work history for better and clearer evidence of your competencies.
8. Work out what you would do differently if you have a similar interview next time.
9. Are you still interested in the job? If so, write a warm thank-you note. It's not too rare that the no. 1 candidate drops out after the job offer stage. You could still be in the frame.
10. Work on your skills. An interview is a performance. Most performances only need practice.

Other self-help books from McGraw-Hill

Take Control of Your Career
Price: £12.99
ISBN: 0077109678
John Lees is a leading British careers coach and regular contributor to *The Times*, *The Guardian* and *Personnel Today*. Drawing on the experience of high performers, it shows you how to overcome mental and physical barriers, make the best visible impact, and negotiate your job content, career advancement and pay. It will help you to get inside the mind of your employer; find out what makes them tick, and how you can use this information to your advantage. The book also examines how to raise and maintain a good profile as well as how to understand and manage other people's perceptions of you, so you can have the career you want.

How to Get a Job You'll Love, 2007/08 edition: A Practical Guide to Unlocking Your Talents and Finding the Ideal Career
Price: £12.99
ISBN: 007711471X
Want a vocation rather than just a job? Feeling stuck in a career rut? *How to Get a Job You'll Love* takes a unique and creative look at career planning. It's written particularly to help those people who have a strong sense that they want to do something purposeful in life, but don't know what. The book helps you to discover what really interests you in life, your hidden skills and your career 'hot buttons'. There are also plenty of tips on interviews, CV writing, and a special section for those just leaving full-time education. John Lees is a leading Career Transition coach and Career Strategist.

Chasing Daylight
Price: £11.99
ISBN: 0071471723
On 24th May, 2005, Eugene O'Kelly stepped into his doctor's office with a full calendar and a lifetime of plans on his mind. Six days later he would resign as CEO of KPMG. His lifetime plans dwindled to 100 days, leaving him just enough time to say goodbye. *Chasing Daylight* is O'Kelly's honest, touching, and ultimately inspirational memoir completed in the three-and-a-half months between his diagnosis with brain cancer and his death in September 2005. It's haunting yet extraordinarily hopeful voice reminds us to embrace the fragile, fleeting moments of our lives – the irreplaceable time we have with our family, our friends and even ourselves.

Revved!: An Incredible Way to Rev Up Your Workplace and Achieve Amazing Results
Price: £8.99
ISBN: 0071465006
From the co-author of *Fish!* comes a powerful new management parable that gives you the secret to motivating people. *Revved!* tells the story of Katie, a department head at MedSol who, with the help of a popular

Chicago radio psychologist, learns how to reconnect emotionally with her people and turn a disorganised, under-motivated department into a supercharged team of go-getters. In the process, Katie also learns how to revitalise both her personal and professional life, and plane new avenues to greater success. A must-read for anyone who wants to have a great time at work!

Life Matters – How to Generate Positive Momentum in Every Aspect of your Life
Price: £14.99
ISBN: 0071422137
As the home front and the work front become increasingly integrated in contemporary life, success – or failure – in either has an undeniable effect on the other. But it is possible to keep both areas moving forward in positive ways. *Life Matters* shows reader how to navigate the critical relationships between time and money, work and family, to create a harmonious, success-enhancing dynamic between each.

Time Management, A Briefcase Book
Price: £11.99
ISBN: 0071406107
Time Management provides hands-on techniques and tools for making every minute count as it dispels myths that can actually cost instead of save valuable time. It helps managers match the right time-saving tool to each situation, reveals secrets for anticipating rather instead of reacting, and explains how any manager can eliminate procrastination.

Tools for Success: A Manager's Guide
Price: £9.99
ISBN: 0077107101
Tools for Success is your one-stop guide to all the essential management tools, which will help you to develop the performance of your team and your organisation. A concise, yet comprehensive book, it provides the complete spectrum of management tools from time management, to problem solving, from six sigma to balanced scorecard.

Harvard Business School Essentials: Negotiation
Price: £14.99
ISBN: 1591391113
Provides practical advice to help any manager broker better deals, and effectively mediate disputes. Discusses a multitude of negotiation topics, including multiparty negotiations, assessing the position of the opposing side, and determining your sources of power and authority in a negotiation. Also, includes useful tips and tools on preparing for negotiation and closing the deal.

Available from all good booksellers, or direct from McGraw-Hill Customer Services Department on Tel +44 (0)1628 502700 or Fax +44 (0)1628 635895. www.mcgraw-hill.co.uk